8714

TROUT FISHING IN RIVERS

TROUT FISHING IN RIVERS

THE FLY AND ITS PRESENTATION

by
Malcolm
Greenhalgh

Illustrated with
photographs

H. F. & G. WITHERBY LTD.

First published in 1987 by
H. F. & G. WITHERBY LTD.
14 Henrietta Street,
London WC2E 8QJ

British Library Cataloguing in Publication Data

Greenhalgh, Malcolm
Trout fishing in rivers: the fly and its
presentation.
1. Trout fishing   2. Fly fishing
I. Title
799.1'755   SH687

ISBN 0-85493-154-6

Filmset in Monophoto 12pt Apollo
and printed in Great Britain by
BAS Printers Limited, Over Wallop, Hampshire

Go, take thine angle, and with practised line,
    Light as the gossamer, the current sweep;
    And if thou failest in the calm still deep,
In the rough eddy may a prize be thine.
Say thou'rt unlucky where the sunbeams shine;
    Beneath the shadow, where the waters creep,
    Perchance the monarch of the brook shall leap—
For fate is ever better than design.
Still persevere; the giddiest breeze that blows,
    For thee may blow with fame and fortune rife;
Be prosperous—and what reek if it arose
    Out of some pebble with the stream at strife,
Or that the light wind dallied with the boughs?
    Thou art successful; such is human life.

Thomas Doubleday. 1818. *Sixty-five Sonnets.*

Contents

Preface

The literature dealing with fishing for trout in rivers seems vast. So why add to it? My first reason is purely personal. I have enjoyed trout fishing so much that I wanted to write about it, and I have enjoyed the writing almost as much as the fishing. It has been something of a self-indulgence. But secondly, despite the wealth of literature on river trouting none could ever be considered the last word on the subject. Nor is this one!

No matter how competent the angler, new problems appear every season that remain to be solved. Such is the fascination of angling. It is as though the top of the mountain recedes as the angler climbs.

In this book I have re-analysed some of the well-known aspects of the subject, looked critically at equipment and methods, suggested some new approaches, and described a few aspects of river trouting that are either novel or less well-known. Thus I hope that this book will be found of use to trout anglers today and will provide them with points for their consideration and discussion. But I do this with a certain degree of reticence for there are many anglers who are much better than I am.

The pleasure to be gained from days by the river, fly-rod in hand, are greatly enhanced if a camera is carried and a diary kept. Then, through the long nights of the winter close season one can look back with pleasure on the successes and analyse the failures.

Suppose, for example, that the trout ignored for several consecutive days the larger duns and fed almost exclusively on a tiny smut that completely defeated you. A common experience on some waters. There is a problem to be solved: but perhaps someone else has provided the answer. A search through the library; a check of the fishing magazines; possibly a letter to the editors of the angling press, explaining the problem and asking readers for suggestions; a chatter with the more experienced members of the fishing club at the A.G.M. Certainly there will be many suggestions made and these, together with your own hunches, can be made ready for the new season. That is how trout-fishing advances. But if you do solve a problem then tell others about it. Pass on your information and discuss it with other anglers. This adds a lot to the pleasure of being a trout fisherman.

This then is my contribution to river trout fishing and I hope that you will enjoy reading it!

Colour Plates

Diagrams and Drawings

Acknowledgements

Many have helped in the production of this book, either directly or indirectly. Former editors Roy Eaton and John Wilshaw of *Trout and Salmon*, Chris Dawn, editor of *Trout Fisherman* and John Bingham, editor of *Shooting Times* have provided me with a great deal of encouragement as they have continued to publish some of my trout fishing observations.

I have been fortunate as an angler having so many friends who have been prepared to discuss fishing problems and techniques, been prepared to argue with me about some of my ideas and have encouraged me in my writing. Especially I must express my gratitude to all members of Bowland Game-Fishing Association, especially Jack Morris, Albert Sanderson, the two Brians (Hoggarth and Wells), Stuart Butcher (surely the greatest living exponent of the northern wet fly), John Bettaney, Phil Holt, Brian Buckley, Bernard Downes, John Dixon (the best all-round game angler I have known), Chris Heap, Tony Hindle, Brian Rafferty, Eric Haygarth, Bill Hopwood, R. J. "Josh" Hodgson. To learn how to fish for trout on all sorts of rivers the facility of a good club is almost essential. Bowland G.-F. A. is such an organisation, with many miles of excellent well-stocked trout fishing on the Rivers Lune, Wenning, Ribble (six different and diverse "beats"), Hodder and Aire, which offers everything from "big river" to spate stream to chalkstream. I would strongly urge those who find river trouting to their liking to seek out, in their home area, such an Association.

I would also like to express my thanks to Jack Norris and Eric Hirst for their willingness to impart advice and ideas.

I am grateful to Lord Home of the Hirsel for providing the Postscript to this book.

Mark Cooper typed the first draft of the book for me quickly and efficiently.

Phill Williams, a great angler, writer and artist, turned my very scruffy cartoons into works of art and provided several of the photographs.

Finally to Geoff Haslam and my son Peter, both outstanding river and stillwater anglers, go my greatest thanks. They fish with me on scores of occasions each year, have produced many good ideas (some of which are contained in this book) and have been the sounding boards for many of my ideas; I have dedicated this book to Peter.

Thank you all.

Malcolm Greenhalgh
Cumbria. February 1987

CHAPTER ONE

Introduction

"In the wilder parts of England, Wales and Scotland there are many regions where practically every burn holds trout . . . For the brownie no water seems too small. . . ."

Kenneth Dawson.
Salmon and Trout in Moorland Streams. 1928.

Fishing for river trout with the fly, which is what this book is mostly about, has a very long history. As far back as the second century AD the Roman writer Claudius Aelianus (in *De Animalium Natura*) described fly fishing for what was presumably a trout in a river in Macedonia. The history of fly fishing for trout in Britain goes back to the 15th century, coinciding with Dame Juliana Berners, work *A Treatyse of Fysshynge wyth an Angle*. It is from that period that the sport of river trout fishing, that we enjoy today, evolved; that evolution being ably described by a huge number of angling writers, many of them contemporary with, and often responsible for, the changes and new inventions that have appeared over the five centuries since the *Treatyse*.

As has proved to be the case in most fields of man's progress, such as medicine, travel and transport, and communications, the advances of human knowledge made since the late 19th century have been as great or greater than all those produced in preceding times. And trout fishing is no exception.

Take some basic items of tackle. For centuries rods were constructed out of bare wood: deal, ash, hazel, juniper, yew, blackthorn and later imported hickory, lancewood, greenheart and bamboo. The scientific precision of the six-sectioned split cane

13

rod was developed in the 1850s (in the U.S.A.) and no sooner had geniuses such as Hiram Leonard and Charles Ritz perfected these during the first half of this century than great leaps forward were made with steel, then fibre glass and, more recently, carbon-fibre and boron-fibre.

Originally lines were made with hair, usually horse-hair, and it was only very slowly, from the 17th century, that silk lines superceded them. In fact John Waller Hills in his excellent, and recently reprinted work *A History of Fly Fishing for Trout* (1921) wrote "But hair lines long survived, for I can recollect them still being used by the old-fashioned at the end of the last century, and no doubt some could be found even now." Since Hill's book we have seen even more precision in line manufacture under the control of the Association of Fishing Tackle Manufacturers and the space-age plastic lines of various very precise tapers and densities.

The cast (or, as most of us call it today, the "leader") of hair was replaced during the 18th and early 19th centuries by silk-worm gut which continued, almost unchanged, for well over a hundred years. In fact, as a child just after the Second War, I can remember using gut and still have, somewhere, some gut casts. But in the last forty years many different brands of nylon monofilament have ousted gut. One has been able to buy no-knot tapered monofilament leaders in recent years and still the tackle industry is not satisfied. Thus we have the very recent appearance of braided nylon leader butts, some designed to float and others to sink, just as we wish.

Hardly one item of the river trout angler's tackle has remained unchanged since the 1940s—the reel is the only example that I can think of, yet even here we have new materials involved in their construction. I wonder what Frederic Halford or G. E. M. Skues, the giants of river trouting in the first half of the 20th century, would say if they could peruse a tackle catalogue from the second half!

But advances have not just been in the implements of trout fishing. So too have great strides been made in the ways these implements are used to entice the trout to leave the water.

Up to about 1850 sunk wet fly reigned supreme throughout the British Isles, fished either upstream or downstream depending upon the opinion of the angler, possibly regional tradition, maybe the direction and strength of the wind. Two, three or more flies were used on the leader and cast somewhat randomly so that the *water* was fished in the hope that a trout (either seen or unseen) would grab one. But then, in the latter half of the 19th century, a massive step was made that resulted in the use of the floating or dry fly. Beyond any doubt Frederic M. Halford was the major developer and innovator of the dry fly style, even though he didn't actually invent the idea. In fact, as early as 1590 Leonard Mascall (in *A Booke of Fishing with Hooke and Line*) was advocating fly bodies that included cork which would float, and Thomas Barker (in *Barkers Delight, or the Art of Angling*, 1657) wrote, "and now I work much of hog's wooll, for I finde it floateth best and procureth the best sport."

However it is certain that the dry fly was a rare beast until Halford came along. And through his four major works *Floating Flies and how to dress them* (1886), *Dry-Fly Fishing in Theory and Practice* (1889), *Dry-Fly Entomology* (1897) and *The Dry-Fly Man's Handbook* (1913) the technique gained in popularity. He defined the essential tackle, method (*always* cast upstream to a single identified trout) and devised a huge number of fly patterns that imitated the natural flies as far as is possible using silk, fur and feather. As I have already inferred much of the tackle that he described has been superceded in recent years. Yet his insistence of casting upstream to an identified fish with an artificial fly that imitates the natural fly on the water still holds good. As far as it goes!

However, as often happens when the virtues of an apparently new idea are promulgated, old ideas are rejected as heresy and the baby is thrown out with the bathwater.

And this is exactly what happened in the regions of Britain where the dry fly technique was most firmly grasped: the southern chalkstreams of Wiltshire, Hampshire, Dorset, Berkshire, Hertfordshire and Buckinghamshire and, further afield Driffield Beck of East Yorkshire and the limestone streams of Derbyshire. If the fly didn't float it was a wet fly and wet flies were damned. The rest of Britain continued largely as it always had, fly fishing being dominated by the old wet fly.

There then appeared on the scene the great G. E. M. Skues

who, initially, was a disciple and friend of Halford. Skues, a lawyer by profession, had a brain that was trained to question and probe. He soon realised that the majority of trout foods, even in the chalkstream, were not taken from the water surface, and that, when trout were feeding beneath the surface dry fly was not only ineffective but inappropriate. He promoted an alternative style to accommodate his researches, nymph fishing.

Following the way of Halford's development of the dry fly, Skues tied his artificial nymphs to imitate as closely as possible the natural nymphs: he created and published scores of nymph patterns, just as Halford had done for the dry fly. Once more he insisted that the artificial nymph should be cast *upstream* to a fish that could be seen feeding, though in this case beneath the surface. Skues described his ideas in several volumes the best being, in my opinion, *Minor Tactics of the Chalk Stream* (1910), *The Way of a Trout with a Fly* (1921), and *Nymph Fishing for Chalk Stream Trout* (1939). These works, together with those of Halford, are essential reading for all serious river trout fishermen.

To the Purist Dry Fly School, led until his death in March 1914 by Halford, the teachings of the Upstream Nymph School led by Skues were blasphemous, even though the latter still insisted on the use of the dry fly when the trout were taking natural flies from the surface and nymphs only when they were not. The argument raged for about forty years and was, at times, harsh and bitter. But I suppose that this was only natural. Most chalksteam anglers were well-educated, literate and articulate men for whom debate and argument was a major pastime. They were all gentlemen and gentlemen of that era had to obey the rules of gentlemanly and sporting behaviour even if to us nowadays they may seem irrational (and unwritten) rules.

In his excellent book *G. E. M. Skues: The Way of a Man with a Trout* (1977) Donald Overfield reproduced the report of a debate held at the Fly Fishers' Club on the issue:

"The years immediately prior to the 1939–45 war gave rise to a rebirth of dry-fly purism and the rigid code of the Halfordian disciples was once more being pressed upon the southern chalk-streams. . . . After all the years of preaching the up-stream nymph Skues must have felt that his life's work was on trial when the committee of the Flyfishers' Club decided that the matter should be put to debate. . . . .

. . . Dr. Mottram maintained that nymph fishing led to the hooking of many undersized fish . . .

. . . Major Phelps . . . it was only here or there than an expert nymph fisherman was at work, and that generally the rivers were flogged by the inexpert Alexandrian. . . .

. . . Mr. Marling agreed with Major Phelps that nymph fishing was safe for experts only, but not for others . . . (!)

. . . The Rev. F. P. Sheriffs . . . fish and fishable water were becoming fewer and scarcer day by day, and that there were already not nearly enough fish to go round. He therefore agreed that fishing with the nymph ought to be abolished . . .

. . . Mr. Norris . . . to fish with the nymph was a sure way to spoil the water . . .

. . . Mr. Myers . . . if the door was open to nymph fishing it was open to illegal fishing of all kinds and could not be shut . . . (!)

. . . Mr. Peck . . . comparatively easy to clear the water of all fish with the nymph and that we should be restricted to floating fly only . . ."

That is what Skues had to face. Incredible!

Eventually the argument of Skues won the day so that today both imitative dry fly and nymph, cast upstream, are allowed on most beats of most chalkstreams. And since then the upstream nymph technique has been greatly modified by Frank Sawyer, river-keeper and angler (in *Keeper of the Stream*, 1952, and *Nymphs and the Trout*, 1958), and Oliver Kite (in *Nymph Fishing in Theory and Practice*, 1963). Once more these two innovative anglers were chalkstream men.

I have spent some time on the development and debate of dry fly and nymph. Partly because (as we shall see through this book) these two techniques are major weapons in the river trout angler's armoury. Partly to give credit where credit is due. Partly to illustrate the fact that heated argument on angling matters is, in hindsight, ludicrous. Is not trout fly fishing the finest sport there is? So brother anglers. When one disagrees with another's point-of-view do so as brothers and not rivals or enemies. But I want also to pose a question. Why were these two important styles developed on *chalk*streams and by *chalk*stream anglers, and why did they largely pass by the rivers of the rest of the British Isles?

What is so special about these chalkstreams? A chalkstream is one that rises from springs that well up on the slopes of chalk downland. The porous rock of the downland acts as a huge reservoir that releases its store of water slowly. Thus the water issuing forth tends to be fairly constant of temperature, extremely clear and of fairly regular volume. Hence the chalkstreams tend not to fluctuate widely in depth: even in prolonged droughts the flow is maintained. Such a constancy of environment provides an ideal habitat for aquatic creatures. At the same time the high mineral salt content and slight alkalinity of the stream water results in huge weed growth which provides a mass of food for the river food web which culminates with the trout and, eventually, the trout angler. Thus for the angler a chalkstream is close to Eden: trout that grow rapidly; huge and diverse hatches of fly; water so clear that it is often possible to watch every movement of the trout below the surface. But such are exceptional amongst British trout streams.

Until very recently chalkstream trout fishing was a prestigious, exclusively upper or middle class hobby. (There are probably some who would say that this still holds good today.) The amount of such chalkstream fishing is relatively small and thus the economic law of "supply and demand" applied. Very few anglers could afford to have a rod on such waters: most were controlled by small, exclusive syndicates and clubs. And many of those fortunate few were quite happy to remain, year after year, on their one beat with just the occasional visit elsewhere. Thus the majority of chalkstream anglers were one-water men. And such was the trout-producing and trout-holding qualities of the major chalkstreams that some syndicates controlled very short lengths, often no more than a few hundred yards or, at most, two or three miles of river. The angler would know his small beat intimately.

For most chalkstream anglers of the Halford-Skues era it was not just a matter of catching a lot of fish. They were inquisitive. They could watch the fish feeding and see their reaction to the fly. They were prepared to experiment to test pet theories. They could discuss and argue over their findings. And being from the better-educated classes these fortunate few spent the long months of the winter close season promoting their Holy Grail. Thus the main developments and the majority of trout fishing literature of the last hundred years came from chalkstream anglers and dealt with the development of the dry fly and nymph.

However, chalkstream angling contrasts greatly with the majority of trout waters as are found in Ireland, Scotland, northern England, Wales and the south-west Peninsula. Regions that have many times more rivers and streams holding brown trout available to the angler than have the southern chalklands. Furthermore, most of the upland regions have a very low density of human population as compared with southern England. Thus there is, going back to the basic premise of economic law, high supply and lower demand. On most upland rivers and streams, therefore, the cost of good trout fishing is relatively inexpensive and angling is embraced by the whole spectrum of humanity. The farm labourer fishes the same water as the farm manager, and the farm manager the same as the estate owner. From the towns of northern England, South Wales and central Scotland the factory worker can afford the best river trout fishing that he may share with his employer. There are few river beats in these upland regions which are, for trout fishing, expensive and exclusive; and where there is expense and exclusivitity it is generally due to the presence of salmon or sea trout in the water. But consider this latter: go to the River Tweed at Kelso where salmon fishing is exclusive and expensive (and often paid for by the wealthy from southern England). Famous beats like Hendersyde, Sprouston, Junction Pool. Yet the outstanding trout fishing on these same waters is available for small cost.

So prolific is trout fishing in much of upland Britain that it hardly mattered at all how the trout were caught, provided the methods used were legal. (I say "were", for increasingly fisheries are imposing restrictions on the methods that can be used.) Fly, spinner, natural minnow, "creeper", worm and maggot: all were widely used and on some beats of some rivers they all still can be used. A far cry from the strict adherence to upstream dry fly and nymph on the chalkstreams.

A large proportion, if not most, of English trout anglers would throw up their hands in protest at the very thought of bait fishing for trout! But many Scottish and Welsh anglers, together with a (diminishing) number in northern England would retort that bait fishing has always been a legitimate way of catching trout. Indeed, as a native of the Pennine streams tradition, on some of the streams that I fish the Rules permit me to use bait as well as fly for brown trout. Through my fishing career I have used all the allowed and recognised bait techniques but, in recent years, have restricted myself more and more to the fly because I enjoy it more than bait fishing and I think that the fly is far more successful on 99% of days. The one exception is when the river is in a roaring flood and the trout might be catchable, with a worm, in the slower pools.

The question that must be asked, not only by those fishery owners who prohibit the use of bait, but also those who permit the use of bait is: "Is the use of bait to catch river trout a reasonably sporting method?"

I know of many instances where wholesale groundbaiting and ledgering with worm and maggot has decimated the trout stocks of clear Pennine streams. I know of at least two instances where spinning the natural minnow has virtually wiped out the trout population of river beats by May so that anglers have had then to wait for the spawning run in summer for the chance of catching a trout. I could give details of a case where numbers of stock fish were caught (and returned) on spinners bearing treble hooks that seem certain to have physically harmed the fish. Or where members of one fishing club, having heard by jungle telegraph that the club having the opposite bank had stocked the river, arrived en masse and camped by the pools until all or most of the stockies had been extracted on ledgered worm.

On the other hand, on fly-only waters I have found, caught up in the branches of a waterside tree, a fly tipped with maggot. I know of many instances where fly fisherman have stolen more than their bag limit and have pursued the stock fish as soon as the fishery wagon has left the river. And I can see no justification for using larger reservoir lures to catch stockies in fly-only rivers. This is no different than using a small spinner.

It is not the method but the angler who is or is not sporting.

A sporting angler is one who puts the fish and fishery first, who will not harm the fishery and who is not constantly concerned about getting his "fair share" of the fish. As to method: a dead trout is a dead trout, no matter how it was taken.

Having said that let me say that I come down heavily on the side of restrictions simply because it is impossible to ensure that all anglers act in a sporting manner. Probably 99% do. But the other 1% can ruin a trout fishery unless their selfishness is controlled. The best way to do this is by having clearly defined restrictions of method. If only trout were inedible, or so abundant that no-one could sell them, or that the deep-freeze had never been invented. But never ever say that fly fishing is more sporting than bait fishing for this infers that the fly fisherman is more of a sportsman than the bait angler. He isn't.

The real difference is that in bait fishing the angler tries to catch the trout on something that they are not naturally feeding on whereas in fly fishing the angler is trying to catch trout on an imitation of what they *are* naturally feeding on. That is what this book deals with.

Whilst a huge volume of literature has been produced about trout fishing on the southern chalkstreams, very very little has emerged from the upland rivers. One reason for this is that the upland rivers are usually spate rivers. Following heavy rain they are turned into dirty raging floods; during droughts they shrink to mere sluggish trickles. They tend to be coloured with suspended clay or the beer-tinge washed from peaty moorlands. And many flow over a catchment area of hard resistant rock so that they tend to be slightly acidic and low in salt content. Thus these rivers rarely produce the huge hatches of fly that are common on the chalkstreams and for much of the time the trout are quite invisible in the murky depths. So most northern anglers do not have the opportunity of watching the reactions of trout to the natural or artificial fly—they simply do not lend themselves to angling research as do the chalkstreams.

But there is another side to it. Most anglers in the upland regions of Britain, certainly in the late 19th and early 20th centuries, were not middle class literate men. They did not argue about methods and mull over new fly patterns. They had no need to. They had a variety of traditional wet flies that had been handed down to them and they backed these up with the use of bait. These methods were effective. So why change things? Hence, with few exceptions (notably T. E. Pritt *North Country Flies*, 1886, Harfield Edmonds and Norman Lee *Brook and River Trouting*, 1916) nothing was heard from the spate rivers whilst the deep south dry fly and nymph revolutions were under way.

In more recent years a new form of trout fishing has flourished: reservoir trout fishing. The traditional stillwater angling of the English Lakes, Welsh llyns, Scottish lochs and Irish loughs has always tended to be a simple extension of the older river wet fly style together with the use of bait. Here the quarry has been wild brown trout and, in some waters, charr and other arctic relict species. However the new stillwater angling is based on the stock-pond rainbow trout, with lesser quantities of stock-pond brown trout and American brook trout (speckled charr). These (especially the rainbow trout) can be raised quickly and cheaply to large size before release. Thus relatively inexpensive fishing has been made available for big trout on so many waters that the majority of trout anglers, certainly in central and southern England, now consider this sort of fishing pre-eminent. The early pioneers of English reservoir fishing, many of whom were chalkstream anglers, could never have envisaged what they started.

On some of the earlier reservoir fisheries restrictions were imposed on fishing methods: dry fly and nymph on some, any fly up to a certain size on others. But on most just about anything was allowed to go provided it was propelled on normal fly tackle and was what could loosely be called a "fly". Soon the majority of reservoir anglers fishing for these stock fish found that the most effective way of obtaining the magic "bag limit" was to use specially designed rods and lines that permitted long-distance casting. And at the end of the line huge, multicoloured lures which were pulled quickly back through the water. Spinning with a fly rod! There is no other word for it. But if the rules allow it, why not?

In the angling press controversy, some of it harsh, bitter and reminiscent of the Nymph Debate that I mentioned earlier, has occasionally erupted over the widespread use of the large lure.

Some reservoir anglers, who are anti-lure, have assumed for themselves the supreme title of "nymph fisherman", a title that puts them on a much higher plane of sportsmanship than their lure-stripping fellows. But go and look at a not untypical reservoir nymph angler's box of "nymphs" and observe how, in general, he fishes them. Tied on size 10 or 8 hooks, many of these so-called nymphs are more than twice the size of the natural. In gaudy colours and touched with fluorescence and glitter. Fished so that they move at speeds such as a yard every 10 seconds: much slower than lures. But how many nymphs are so big, so glittering and swim even that fast. Surely these nymphs are also lures. But they certainly catch a lot of stocked trout!

It is this style that has dominated the trout angling literature for the past two decades. How to catch reservoir trout. How to catch the really big rainbow.

Throughout the boom in angling literature based on the chalk-stream and the completely different literature on the English stillwater concept there has been far less written on the majority of British trout fishing (possibly after Scottish lochs and Irish loughs), river trouting. So this book is written in an attempt to fill the gap. To bring together the dry fly and nymph methods of the chalkstream with the tiny wet flies that have stood the test of time on the northern and western streams. To look at river trout fishing from the point-of-view of the spate stream angler and link this with the chalkstream. And whereas most early chalkstream anglers and writers fished, in the main, one beat or one river, I have drawn the majority of my experiences from the following: Nith, Annan, Eden, Rawthey, Lune, Wenning, Ribble, Hodder, Aire, Wharfe, Ure, Tees, Tyne, Tweed, Teviot, Spey, Dovey, Dysynni, Dwyfor as well as some other smaller streams in the Hebrides, mainland of Scotland, North Wales, Devon, Derbyshire, the West Riding of Yorkshire, Lancashire and Cumbria.

CHAPTER 2

Tackle for River Trout

"All rods can catch fish: their success depends on the hand that uses them. But there are rods and rods! Good ones are rare. . . . A faultless rod is one of the best trump-cards a fisherman has for attaining his goal."

Charles Ritz. *A Fly Fisher's Life*. 1959.

On the opening day of a recent trout season Peter and I were walking back to the car. By a large pool was a new club member who seemed to be having a problem with his casting. From his casting action it was clear that he needed some coaching.

"This is new to me," he commented. "I don't know if I will ever master it!"

"Well," I began. "Your casting could easily be improved. Shall I show you where you are going wrong?"

He was only too eager to learn. So he passed me his rod and I proceeded to cast, or, rather, attempted to proceed to cast to show him how to throw out a delicate line. But to no avail! As I flicked the line on the forward cast the middle of the rod waggled about and all I achieved was the most awful zig-zag splashy cast of a very moderate distance. I looked at the rod. It had the best reel fittings and rings. I looked at the reel: it was a reasonable make. There seemed nothing wrong with the line. I looked at the rod again: there was no maker's name, nor any other marking.

I turned to Peter and asked him to put up my rod so that I could demonstrate casting on a set of reasonable tackle. Then I turned to the new member.

"Oh yes!" he replied to my query. "It's carbon fibre."

"Where did you buy it?"

"A special offer".

"It only cost £45 with all the rest of the stuff in a kit!"

Now analyse this bargain bit by bit. At the time the reel fitting and rod rings had a retail value of at least £6; the line £8.35; the reel £16.58. Total £30.98.

He paid £45 for the whole kit. Thus the rod blank, the part that does the actual work of propelling the fly-line out across the water and the fly to the fish cost at most £14.07. Take off the cost of the free flies and cast (free!) and the manufacturer's and retailer's profit and what had he really bought? Probably less than ten pounds-worth of man-made rubbish.

This kit seemed inexpensive. It wasn't. It was cheap *and expensive*! For the purchaser of such a piece of rubbish must either abandon the sport of fly fishing, in which case he has lost £45 and the chance of partaking in the world's finest hobby, or he must go out and spend even more of his hard-earned cash on a good rod. In this latter case the loss is not so great. The reel can be used; possibly the line. The good-quality rings and reel fittings can be removed from the horrid nasty rod so that they can be re-used on either a good-quality rod blank or as spares. So far the loss is now only £14.07. The two pieces of the denuded "rod" can then be used as supports for plants in the herbaceous border. Expensive canes!

To the beginner to trout fishing I can give no better advice than this.

"Look gift horses in the mouth!"

"There really is no such thing as a bargain!"

It might be thought that this instance was a "one-off" and that it won't happen to you. Why? These advertisers are all reputable dealers. Aren't they?

The vast majority of tackle dealers are reputable. But most of us have been stung at one time or another by the lure of cheap tackle. I bought a bargain reel that came to pieces on the second day out. That was it! I was 30 miles from my reel cupboard and the trout were feeding keenly. Ten pounds for the reel, plus petrol money, plus a day's fishing lost. I went back to the supplier of the offending reel to ask for my money back. Alas, the supplier had been declared bankrupt! So, go to a reputable dealer for your tackle and buy the best that you can afford by a manufacturer who has a high standard, reputation and long-established name to live up to.

The fishing tackle industry offers an immense range of each item of tackle that a fly-fisher will need: rods, reels, lines, leader material, hooks, landing-nets etc. etc. To a newcomer to the sport, a bewildering range. To the old-hand, who has been using the same set of trusted tried tackle for years, an unnecessarily complicated proliferation.

Much of the growth in weight of the tackle catalogues and their wares are only a small extent due to an attempt to lure the angler into buying something that he doesn't really need or that are of no consequence. Some manufacturers have tried to jump on some band-wagon and marketed frivolities or gimmicks. Such have usually been an abysmal failure, both for the manufacturer and, even worse, the poor angler who has fallen for them. Other items have been produced in an attempt to provide for those who seek a bargain—cheaper pieces than the standard production models that are usually less efficient from the start and have a short life expectancy. The majority of the contents of the tackle catalogue, however, are there because either they have stood the test of time or, increasingly, the result of innovation or improvement brought about by the advancement of science. They are the result of the progress that I spoke of in the Introduction.

So in this chapter I will look at river trout fishing tackle: old well-proven pieces, recent improvements, new innovations. I will point out some pitfalls that the new angler may fall into when he sets forth to equip himself. I will give my opinion, as far as it is worth, on what is available.

I must explain, before I begin, that over recent years I have "tried out" a huge amount of tackle that either I or one of my friends have purchased. I have no financial interest whatsoever in the tackle trade other than an angler who must buy the tools of his trade. Recommendations given are given freely.

Rods
Over the years river trout rods have been made from a wide variety of materials: ash, lancewood, greenheart, split cane, steel, solid fibre glass, hollow fibre glass, carbon fibre and boron. In

recent years only three of these have been regarded seriously by river trout anglers: cane, carbon (known as graphite by manufacturers in the United States and Japan) and boron. Some anglers still use hollow fibre glass but the advent of carbon and boron has made this material obsolete as far as fly rods are concerned (though some are still marketed).

Before considering the relative merits of the three rod materials it must be stressed that, generally, in river trout fishing delicacy and accuracy of the cast are of paramount importance and *not* distance. There is rarely the need to cast more than ten yards or so. Compare this with the quite usual reservoir cast of thirty yards plus. Thus the tackle used on a reservoir will not be effective on a river or stream.

The typical reservoir rod: usually takes a heavy line (Association of Fishing Tackle Manufacturers No. 8 or more); needs a lot of line outside the rod tip if the rod is going to work properly and is thus quite ineffective on very short casts; lends itself to heavy casting, is associated with tackle such as the weight forward line or shooting head line and the style of casting known as double-hauling; is often used over deep water where there is less chance of disturbing the fish with splashy casts.

The typical river trout rod: must be able to cast a light line of AFTM 7, preferably 6 or 5 or less; must be able to cover trout that are very close, often no more than five yards away; must be able to deliver the cast delicately to fish that are in very shallow, often clear, water; must be able to cast into a stiff breeze (the reservoir angler can use his boat or move round the bank to alleviate a strong headwind); must enable accurate casting. It must be able to place the fly in really awkward positions—under overhanging branches or low foot bridges, between branches, over grass tussocks etc. In the hands of a competent angler the fly should land on a sixpence at ranges up to ten yards. It must be positive on the strike when using small hooks (rarely does the reservoir angler use hooks of size 14 and less yet these are the typical sizes for the river).

27

Of all these delicacy and accuracy of casting are the major requirements. I must stress the fact that river trouting is a completely different game from reservoir trouting: certainly as far as most people fish reservoirs. Yet occasionally I meet anglers on the small streams using completely inappropriate reservoir tackle.

So what rod or rods?

On balance my recommendation is to obtain a good split-cane rod which will last for life. And there are, on the market, three excellent models, that I have used so I can testify to their outstanding quality.

Sharpes Featherweight 8′ 6″ AFTM6.   My son Peter has used this for all of his river fishing since he was thirteen years of age. It is a fine rod for short distances and very accurate.

Sharpes Scottie 9′ AFTM6.   Several of my angling friends use one of these for medium-sized or larger rivers where casts of up to twenty yards are sometimes needed. It is a powerful rod, yet casts a delicate and accurate line.

Sharpes Eighty Eight 8′ 8″ AFTM5/6.   The most expensive of the three I have listed but beyond doubt the best cane rod on the market, especially for upstream nymph and dry fly fishing.

These cane rods may seem expensive, but they are no more expensive than a good quality rod made in carbon fibre or boron. Furthermore they are as robust as any man-made material in that the cane is specially hardened and waterproofed by a process of impregnation. Thus they never need re-varnishing, as did many other makes of cane rod, nor do they suffer the problem of bending or "setting" as was always the problem of older cane rods. These rods are still on the market because they have stood the test of time.

However, the most popular rod material nowadays is carbon-fibre and this has certain merits over split-cane in river trouting. Carbon rods are much lighter. Thus whereas a full day wet fly fishing with a cane rod can raise blisters and cause seg formation on the inside of the fingers and on the palm of the hand, especially at the beginning of a new season, this rarely happens when carbon rods are used non-stop throughout the day. However, as we shall see throughout the rest of this book dogged non-stop casting should have little part in river trouting. The lightness of the carbon-fibre rod also allows much longer rods to be used on rivers which enables the angler to utilize a much higher back cast to avoid fences, bushes and banks behind him that would hinder the backcast of a shorter rod. Carbon rods are also usually stiffer and more powerful, thus crisper and more accurate casts are possible.

It is the stiffness of the carbon rod that is, to my mind, its greatest drawback. Being so relatively stiff, the angler does not feel quite as in touch with a fish hooked on carbon as he is with one on split-cane. Thus some of the pleasure and thrill of playing a trout is removed by the carbon rod.

Even more troublesome is that the less-elastic power of carbon-fibre can result more easily in a breakage of the leader point when the strike is made or when the fish takes a sudden lunge on a very tight line. With a cane rod the top joint cushions the strike and sudden jerky movements by the fish. The rod just bends. Such a rod allows the angler to use very fine leader points (as low as two pounds breaking strain) which is of great value when the river is low and clear, and the trout easily disturbed. With a carbon-fibre rod breakages of the leader point are more common and can be successfully remedied only by using a heavier nylon point (possibly four pounds breaking strain) or by incorporating a short length of elastic "Shock Gum" into the leader butt (see p. 37).

Hence my own first choice is a cane rod. One can use a finer leader point. Thus over the years more fish will be hooked. And the sensitivity of the cane will mean less fish being lost due to the hold being torn away or the leader point failing.

> *Note:* For salmon, sea trout and reservoir trout fishing, where continuous long casting is generally the order of the day, cane rods are unsuitable and have been superceded by carbon and boron rods.

However, carbon rods are with us and I often use them especially on larger rivers where a longer cast may be necessary, when the river is high following rain and I tend to use a stronger leader point, or when fishing in the twilight. Some very experienced anglers now use nothing else. A testimonial for carbon rods could come from no better source than Jack Norris, probably the best dry fly fisherman in northern England, who has, in recent years, abandoned split-cane in favour of this new material.

The thorny problem, as far as the novice to river trouting is concerned, is which carbon rod to buy. There are so many. Just about every major retailing company of fly fishing tackle has a series of rods carrying their own brand name and advertisements in the angling press swarm with them! How can the famous manufacturers, who sell through these same retail outlets, hope to compete? The answer is quality. You get what you pay for.

Therefore the great names of rod manufacture should be seriously considered when purchasing a new rod even though their rods might cost significantly more than the retailer's own brand or less famous makes. Of the carbon-fibre rods I have used the following are great river trout rods:

Orvis Limestone 8' 6" AFTM6
Orvis Hampshire 9' AFTM6
Hardy De-Luxe Graphite 9' AFTM5/6
Hardy Favourite Graphite 9' 3" AFTM4/5
Bruce and Walker Century 11' 3" AFTM4/6

Note: Some anglers might argue that the length of the latter is ridiculous on rivers where brown trout rarely scale much more than a couple of pounds. But think of it this way. A long rod will do what a short rod will do and more besides. Long rods allow for a higher backcast. They allow for more of the line being held out of the water during the actual fishing of the fly and thus help to reduce the problem of "drag" which, as we shall see later, is one of the biggest headaches of the river trout angler. They allow for the line to be held higher during the playing of the trout so that there is more control over the hooked fish.

If these rods are beyond the budget then there are two alternatives. The first is to go to a reputable dealer and let him kit you out with his own brand of tackle or, possibly, with one of the lesser manufacturer's products. But remember. There are two sorts of tackle dealers: the one who wants to take your money and see you leave the shop as quickly as possible and the sort who is only too happy to give you time and advice whilst you make your choice. Sometimes the latter will even let you try out the rod or whatever before you make your final decision.

A second alternative for effective cost-cutting, yet maintaining good quality, is to purchase rod blank, rod rings, handle and reel-fitting separately and either do-it-yourself or have someone do-it-for-you. I have several such rods, all of which are superb, made from blanks manufactured by North West Blanks Ltd. and Fibatube Ltd. Such rods cost less than half that of an equivalent full rod and, because one has purchased the individual components, one can make a rod exactly to one's liking. The only disadvantage, if such it be, of roll-your-own rods is that they never command the sort of second-hand price that do manufactured rods. But how many anglers buy a rod to sell it!

Some might say that there is also the disadvantage that should failure or breakage occur in roll-your-own rods one cannot go back to the manufacturer. True. But every angler should have adequate insurance to cover replacement costs of all his fishing tackle at home, in the car and on the river.

The third rod material, boron, is a light material, as is carbon, but is said not to have the mechanical problems of carbon fibre. During the 1970s and early 1980s the angling press published many articles and letters dealing with the reputation of carbon fibre rods—that they were "notch-sensitive" (i.e. a slight nick in the wall of the rod would probably result in the rod shattering violently). I have been using carbon fly rods for over ten years now; I have seven of them. Never have I had a breakage and nor, to my knowledge, have any of my angling acquaintances. Therefore I think the problem, if problem it be, has been grossly exaggerated. Drop a rod onto boulders, fall on it, use it for flattening the nettles or prodding jackdaw nests from the chimney and it is quite likely to break. Used properly there seems not to be a problem.

However, boron rods were hailed, in the early 1980s, as an improvement over carbon. They were said not to have this shattering problem, less stiff than carbon yet as powerful. I have tried two different boron rods on the river and find no real advantage in them. However, there are fewer boron rods on the market and most of them are built for heavy work on reservoirs: too heavy for river work.

31

Lines

Sooner or later a newcomer to the world of river trout fishing will bump into an old hand who still uses dressed silk lines. The novice will be told, of silk lines, that "you can't beat 'em . . . they are smoother to shoot . . . they are much finer than plastic lines . . . !"

There is a grain of truth in such comments. But a little grain. Quite honestly, though many of my angling friends use them and will be quite horrified in what I am going to say, the use of silk lines today is something of an affectation, for the standard of *the best* plastic-coated modern fly lines is extremely high. Let me compare the two:

Traditional Silk Line:

Advantages

Finer in diameter, shoots well, less water disturbance

Disadvantages

Needs regular (daily) annointing with grease

In scummy water tends to sink

Must be stripped from the reel and dried after use

Prone to rotting

More expensive than the best modern lines

Modern Plastic Coated Line:

Advantages

Needs little maintenance (see later)

Good flotation

Will not rot

Can be left on the reel from day to day and from season to season

Less expensive

Consistent—a new line of a certain specification will be identical to the old line

Disadvantages

Marginally thicker in diameter and therefore may be slightly more splashy when landing on the water than silk lines.

So, on balance, use modern plastic coated lines as do the vast majority of modern anglers.

Such plastic lines come in a variety of sorts and sizes and it is not my intention to go into this here. There are many references to which the reader can turn that explain the variety of such lines. All that the river trout angler will need is one, possibly two, and if he is really keen three lines. These are:

Double Taper Floating   *ESSENTIAL*
Double Taper Slow Sinking   *USEFUL SOMETIMES*
Double Taper Sink Tip/Anti-skate   *NICE TO HAVE*

As the names suggest, all are tapered at either end. Thus when one end (the end which is used on each cast and to which the leader is attached) becomes worn, the line can be reversed so that, in theory, the line has a double life. I get about 150 days fishing from one end of a double taper line and, in practice, slightly less (say 100 days) from the other end. This is equivalent to three or four years of life of the floating line.

The vast majority of river trouting involves the floating line. But when fishing fairly deep slow pools, fast deep runs of the spate river when it is high after heavy rain, the sinker or sink tip can be used to good effect to get the *wet fly* deep to where the fish are. But these lines are of no use for nymph or dry fly fishing.

Now for weight of line. A good rod should have marked on it, usually above the handle, the recommended AFTM standard for that rod. The larger the AFTM number the heavier the line. Thus the number 5/6 means that the rod works best with either size 5 or 6 lines. Ideally the angler will have purchased a rod for river trouting that will handle lines of AFTM 5 or 6. Apropos of what was said earlier about the unsuitability of reservoir tackle for river fishing, most modern reservoir rods take much heavier lines.

There can be no compromise. Trying to cast a light line on a rod constructed to take a heavy line is frustrating, for the line will not work the rod properly and casting will be ineffective. Likewise, trying to fish with a heavy line on a light rod will overstrain the rod and produce horrible casts. The purchase of rod and line must go hand in hand and with due regard to the water to be fished. Thus for these purchases the offices of a good tackle dealer are essential.

When it comes to choosing a line the beginner has a bewildering choice. Suppose he wants a DT6F (double taper, size 6, floater). One mail order firm advertised, in April 1983, fourteen different types, colours and makes: floating and high floating, mill ends, cheap specials, supremes.

Remember that you get what you pay for and that there is a noticeable difference, when fishing, between a cheap floater and an expensive floater. For instance, the better floaters do float, if looked after, for their entire life. Cheap ones often don't, especially at the tip, from Day One.

As to the colour. Some people say that it is irrelevant and others that it is important. I am persuaded that it does matter when conditions are hard (on clear water streams or during summer droughts on spate rivers) and thus I like dull green or brown lines, sink or float. There is one exception, when I am fishing overnight in summer and then I like a white line that is more visible in the gloaming.

And some makes that I can recommend:

Alas McKenzie-Philps (Wetherby) have ceased trading*. Their Yorkshire Floating Fly line was the best I have used.
Aircel Supreme Mahogany Floater
Aircel Wet Tip Anti Skate
Wet Cel No. 1 Slow Sink
Masterline Chancellor Green Floater
Masterline Chancellor Sink

Care of the Floating Fly Line: The plastic coating loses its suppleness and begins to crack on even the best lines in time. To prevent this and guarantee perfect flotation carry out the following drill after every ten to twenty days fishing.

Strip the line from the reel into a sink of luke warm water to which has been added a little liquid detergent. Allow ten minutes soaking time and then wipe dry with a soft clean cloth. You will be surprised how dirty the line will be. Then take some *Permagrease* and give the line a good coating. Permagrease is not only a water-repellant (so it aids line flotation) but it also contains a line plasticiser than helps the line retain its suppleness. Carry Permagrease with you to the river and should the tip of the fly line show signs of sinking, give it a quick application. By so doing you will add to the life span of your fly lines.

*The 1987 *Fishermens Feathers Catalogue*. This firm now sells most of the excellent McKenzie-Philps products. Their address is: Fishermens Feathers, Crowan, Nr. Camborne, Cornwall TR14 9NB.

Reel

In fly fishing the reel is a convenient store of line. Occasionally it can be used when playing a fish, but more usually the fish is played by hand, pulling line in and letting it fall onto the water or on the bank at one's feet. Thus the construction of the fly reel is, typically, a simple one that is, basically, unchanged from the ones in use half a century or more ago. However there are a lot of reels on the market that have been produced by cutting corners to reduce costs. Poor spindle bearings, frail and fragile checks, poor line guard or no line guard at all so that fly lines are quickly damaged, weak plastic or very soft alloy construction so that the slightest knock ruins them, screws that go missing and the reel falls to bits, soldered or rivetted joints that break irreparably. Such seem common in a lot of cheap modern reels. So a reliable reel that will give years of service will be less expensive, in the long run, than many bargains.

Some reels have gears so that one turn of the handle will give several turns of the reel drum, thus increasing the rate of line-retrieve.

There are, also, some automatic reels, which by pushing a lever, rapidly reel in slack line. They have the disadvantage of greater weight. I have never used one, but Peter McKenzie-Philps uses and recommends them, so perhaps they are worthy of consideration.

The following are, in my opinion the best of the various types on the market, bearing in mind not only quality but also cost:

Ungeared

    Hardy Perfect $3\frac{3}{8}''$
    Hardy Marquis $3\frac{1}{4}''$ } —expensive but outstanding

    Shakespeare Beaulite $3\frac{1}{2}''$ } —moderate price
    J. W. Young 1500 Series $3\frac{1}{2}''$ }   but excellent

Geared

    Shakespeare Speedex $3\frac{1}{2}''$
    J. W. Young 1500 Series $3\frac{1}{2}''$ Geared } —fine reels!

Where the angler has several lines then he has the option of buying several reels or one reel with several spare spools to match. Considering the relative inexpense of the spare spool the latter seems to be financially the best option. However, for some types of angling it is of advantage to have two rods set up so that the angler can change from one method to another without having to reassemble his rods during fishing. For example in spring I like to have two rods set up, one with a team of wet flies and one with dry fly; in summer evenings when I fish for sea trout I have two rods set up, one with sinking line and one with a floater. On those occasions two reels and, of course, two rods are essential.

Backing Line

This line provides a means of attaching fly line to reel and is an insurance should a particularly large fish take the fly and make powerful runs beyond the capacity of the fly line. Rarely do river brown trout take so much line that a lot of backing is needed but once, on the River Spey, I hooked a $3\frac{1}{2}$ lb. brownie that made over 60 yards on its first run in double-quick time. Try to stop such a run dead, and either the hook-hold will tear away or the fine nylon leader point will break. And one must remember that in some brown trout streams there may also be salmon and sea trout that do, on occasion, take tiny wet flies. You may never need a lot of backing when river trouting: but if you do, boy, do you need a lot of it! Better to be prepared and land that really big trout rather than trail home sadly saying, "if only"!

There is one other function of backing line. A near empty reel spool requires far more turns of the handle to pull in, say, ten yards of line than if the spool is full. Thus the spool should have enough backing so that, with the fly line, it is full.

Special braided backing line can be bought but it is expensive. The easiest, least expensive and as efficient sort of backing line is heavy monofilament. I use cheap sea-angling line of 30 lbs. B.S. and with a jumbo spool of 1000 metres of such line there is enough backing for at least five fly lines.

Leaders

Most of us have, for years, been using home-made leaders, made by knotting together appropriate lengths of monofilaments of different diameters and strengths. Under no circumstance try to get away with using a uniform length of plain nylon: this will not turn over properly in the cast and tangles will result.

Make-up for nine foot leader

21″	9″	9″	9″	12″	4′	Tip of Fly Line
4lb. B.S.	6lb	8lb	10lb	15lb	20lb	

Point Fly	Middle Dropper	Top Dropper

Note: Each dropper is 4–6″ long, of 4lb B.S. monofilament. In upstream dry fly fishing or nymph fishing no droppers are used.

For river fishing for trout a nine foot leader is ideal, made up as follows:

4 feet of	20 lb. B.S. nylon
12 inches of	15 lb. B.S. nylon
9 inches of	10 lb. B.S. nylon
9 inches of	8 lb. B.S. nylon
9 inches of	6 lb. B.S. nylon
21 inches of	4 lb. B.S. nylon—the leader point

If a 6 lb. B.S. point is required then use 21 inches of the 6 lb. line. If a lighter point is required then reduce the 4 lb. B.S. length to nine inches and attach a 21-inch point of appropriate lower B.S. to that. If a leader of more or less than nine feet is required, increase or decrease respectively the 20 lb. and 15 lb. B.S. lengths in a 4:1 ratio to give the new leader length.

When wet fly fishing it is common practice to use one or two droppers so that the trout have the choice of two or three flies. (Some Scottish anglers employ even more droppers!) If one dropper is needed then use one of 4 lb. B.S. at the junction between the 4 lb. point and the 6 lb. B.S. length. Thus the point fly and dropper will be about 21 inches apart. Then if a third fly (or second dropper) is required attach it about three feet above the first dropper (i.e. to the length of 15 lb. B.S. nylon). The droppers should be between four and six inches long.

Earlier I mentioned the problem of the leader point snapping during the strike or when a biggish trout makes a strong run (p. 29). This is especially likely when very light leader points are being used and/or very stiff rods that do not cushion the force of the fish. To avoid this *Shock Gum* could be incorporated into the leader.

Shock Gum is a fairly stiff fine form of elastic that will stretch sufficiently to prevent very light leader-points shattering. A short length (I have found about six inches satisfactory) is tied in at the base of the leader. Most anglers never use it: but it is well worth trying if you are suffering from a spell of breaking on fish or when getting used to a new rod.

Tapered leaders　In recent years the tackle trade has improved on plain monofilament for leaders by producing special tapered leaders that act as an extension of the fly line and are, of course, knotless. Such bought leaders "turn over" much better in the cast than knotted leaders and the lack of knots greatly reduces the chance of tangles.

Tapered nylon leaders come in a wide range of size to suite all styles of fly fishing and it is important to ensure, when buying them, that the correct size is bought for the job in hand. Such leaders have three apparent disadvantages over home-made knotted ones:

1. they are expensive compared with spools of nylon.
2. because of the high cost there is the temptation to use them until they are well and truly worn out. Thus there is the risk of losing a good trout due to a weakened leader point.
3. as the leader becomes shorter as old flies are removed and new ones tied in place, so either the whole must be scrapped or a new point of level monofilament tied on the end.

This latter is, however, not a disadvantage at all when used with forethought. Some years ago I was on a fishing holiday with Ken Clapperton and Ronnie Cowgill. They used knotless tapered leaders, permanently attached to the fly line with a superglued needle-knot. Once the fine point was too short they simply attached a new one from a spool of nylon. Thus they had a tapered leader butt very reminiscent of the new braided ones (see below) with just the one knot where the point was attached compared to several knots along a home-made knotted leader. Ken gave me one to try: I found it an excellent leader, far superior to my own.

For river trout fishing I would recommend the Leeda Platil Cast, without droppers, 3 lb. B.S. Point.

Braided Leader Butts Even more recently we have seen the invention of the tapered braided leader butt which has almost done away with the need for monofilament leaders.

These fit snuggly over the end of the fly line and taper down to a fine diameter end onto which one ties a leader point of appropriate breaking strain. I have used them since their introduction and recommend them to all trout anglers.

Braided leaders appear very expensive, but they are not really. One will remain in place for up to two seasons before it has to be replaced (I have one on my DT6F that has been used now for 116 full days fishing and has removed the need for me to knot together bits of nylon). And all I need take to the river is a single spool of nylon just in case I need to attach a new point.

For river trouting I would recommend:

Diamondback Leader 5′

Bob Church Floating Leader 4–6 (to fit lines AFTM 4–6)

Full details of how to attach them are provided.

Flies

These are the most important component of the entire tackle set-up for it is these that attract and hold onto the fish. Most of this book revolves around the trout fly, and chapter 4 gives a list of recommended flies.

Many trout anglers purchase their flies from tackle shops or via mail order. A lot of shop-bought flies are very poor, using awful hooks, third rate materials and are not exactly true-to-type. So beware! Go to a good tackle firm or professional tyer. Ask about their hooks and the materials they use. Order one or two patterns, a few of each, and check them for consistency of quality. Then, if your are satisfied, send them your "wants" list. Some they will be able to provide from their stock; others may have to be tied specially for you.

But there is no better way than to tie your own flies. You can use the best hand-picked materials. You can experiment with new patterns to suit new situations that you have encountered. Your own flies will often be better than shop-bought flies. And, it might be argued, home-made flies are cheaper (this is *not* true, for most home-tyers produce far more flies than they need and end up giving a lot of them away!). So, *learn to tie your own flies*!

39

I learnt from books. Better still go to your local Adult Education Centre. Many of them have evening classes in fly-tying during the winter months, often taught by really expert fly-tyers.

And if you tie your own flies do use the best materials, especially hooks. After many years of trying this hook and that I have finally settled for the British hooks manufactured by Partridge. This firm offers a wide range, some quite special types designed for a particular sort of fly and others quite standard, and their quality control is excellent. Many anglers may point out that Partridge hooks are more expensive than most others. But what is a few pence, if it improves the chances of landing a good trout, when put against the cost of the rest of the tackle, petrol to drive to the river and permit charge?

Try the following:
Captain Hamilton Standard M/W Wet Fly: for all wet fllies
Partridge Mayfly Hook: for mayfly, daddy-long-legs and large
    sedges
Captain Hamilton Nymph Hooks: for nymphs
Captain Hamilton Dry Fly Hooks: for standard dry flies
Swedish Dry Fly Hooks: for superb upside-down dry flies
Sedge Hooks: for realistic imitations of sedge pupae

Recently there has been a great interest in barbless hooks, especially on waters that may contain under-size trout or salmon parr or where the angler wishes to return the fish he catches. Many anglers have been reluctant "to go barbless", fearing that they will lose a lot of big fish. This fear is groundless. Barbless hooks penetrate the jaw of the trout better than hooks with a barb and, provided the fish is kept on a tight line, losses are no greater than is the case with barbed hooks.

Certainly a barbless hook causes less damage to the trout. It is easier to shake gently a fish from a barbless hook and there is no need to handle fish that are to be returned. So give barbless hooks a try! Either de-barb the hook with snipe-nosed pliers or buy some barbless hooks:

Hooper Barbless Dry Fly Down-eyed ⎫ for all nymphs, wet
Captain Hamilton Dry Fly Barbless ⎬ flies and dry flies
J. G. Upside-Down Hooks: for barbless upside-down dry flies

Leader Sinkant

Nylon leader material easily picks up oils from the river water or grease from the hands. And on shallow pools in bright light or on very clear streams a floating leader dimpling the surface and glinting in the sun certainly puts the fish down. So a degreaser or sinkant is required. Most anglers ignore this little item and fail to catch what they should because of their carelessness.

Easy to make: mix "Fairy Liquid" washing-up liquid with Fuller's Earth powder (obtainable at most chemist's) to produce a creamy paste. This is smeared along the leader as and when needed.

Dry Fly Flotant

The late and great Richard Walker invented "permaflote": it is almost essential though some anglers do without, relying on the fly hackle to aid flotation.

A Useful Tip: Dunk your flies in the flotant at home and let them dry out before putting them in the dry fly box. They will then float much better than when the flotant is added immediately before use. Then, when you have caught a fish put the old messy fly away in a box and tie on a fresh one. At home, that evening, wash all used flies in luke warm water. Let them dry and retreat them with flotant. Your dry flies will last much longer when you do this and they will always float.

Landing Net

For trout fishing there is nothing to beat a folding net with extendable handle, that clips onto the fishing bag or belt. Always have one with a non-knotted mesh bag which does not damage a fish should you wish to return it to the water. Indeed, in the Yorkshire Water Authority Region one *must* use a knotless net.

Towards the end of playing a trout, the landing net should be held low in the water at arm's length and then the beaten fish simply led or pulled over it unawares. The net is then raised to lift the trout from the water. All too often, however, it is a misused item of tackle. It comes into play too late so that the dry mesh floats, creating a conspicuous dark bulge which frightens the trout (a pebble dropped in the net before angling

41

commences is often helpful). And all too often, the net is used as a scoop being poked in the trout's direction whenever it gets anywhere near. This often causes the trout to panic. These are common causes of losing trout, especially large trout.

Priest
If you are going to kill a fish then do so humanely, with a heavy priest. An angler who does not carry a suitable priest ought to be evicted from the river bank.

Marrow Spoon
G. E. M. Skues, thought of the idea of using a marrow spoon to extract the stomach contents.

It is often valuable knowing, as soon as possible, what the trout are feeding on, especially beneath the surface. With a "marrow spoon" one can extract the stomach contents of a trout that one has just caught, float the contents in a little bowl of river water and get the answer immediately. There are several excellent marrow spoons on the market that are incorporated into a priest: a two-in-one tool.

Artery Forceps
All anglers should carry a pair of these to remove hooks that are awkwardly attached in a fish or one's person. They can also be used to remove a hook barb should one have to (because of fishery rules) or want to fish barbless.

Clothing
Modern developments have produced two great improvements. The first is the *Polaroid Sunglasses* that greatly enhance underwater vision as well as providing comfort in bright weather.

The second is the new form of fishing jacket. For many years most anglers have been wearing the popular oiled cotton jackets of various makes, none of which seems to remain waterproof for more than a couple of seasons. Even the "re-proofing" does not solve the problem. What is even worse, for the fly fisherman, is that these jackets quickly wear through in the creases on the casting arm.

A couple of years ago Geoff Haslam turned to the new *York-*

shire Jacket and discovered the perfect angling jacket. At the same time I bought yet another waxed cotton jacket. The former is as waterproof as it was on the day it was bought; the latter has been re-waxed and still leaks. Let me recommend the Yorkshire Fishing Jacket, produced by Rainbow All-Weather Clothing and retailed through Fishermens Feathers Ltd.

Alas there has not been much of an improvement in wader durability! It is high time that the wellington boot and thigh wader manufacturers produced a wader that did not perish in less than a couple of seasons. And at a reasonable cost.

Miscellaneous
Spare nylon, scissors, food, drink. A torch if you are going to be fishing all night. All these fit into the traditional fishing bag with spare reel, fly boxes etc.

What to do with the fish you catch? Do not wrap them up in a modern plastic carrier bag or they will have deteriorated by the time you get them home. Use either: an old-fashioned wicker creel or a modern fish bass, both of which keep the fish cool.

What to do about mosquitos and midges? They can spoil the evening hatch in late spring and summer. It is worth being prepared. I use Jungle Formula Mijex and it really works. These irritating pests treat lesser concoctions as a form of salad-dressing!

*   *   *

At this point I must explain that neither details of casting techniques nor how to put up the tackle/tie knots are included in this book. Such information can be found in many books on trout fishing. I would make two recommendations: —to learn the art of casting one ought to go to a qualified professional instructor. Then one will learn how to cast well without the flaws to be found in the casting of so many of us self-taught fly fishermen.
— check and
doublecheck every knot one ties. Many many fish are lost because a shoddily-tied knot has slipped.

CHAPTER 3

River Invertebrates

"During the past one hundred years angling entomology
has become complicated . . . the study of [trout] flies has
now become more highly specialised, and in order to be con-
versant with modern literature on the subject it is necessary
to have a certain amount of technical knowledge."

J. R. Harris. *An Angler's Entomology.* 1952.

In the evolution of the river trout angler there are several possible
stages culminating in the good all-round exponent of the art. The
first is the novice. He goes to the river with his new fishing tackle
together with a series of flies that were recommended by some
tackle dealer or a friend. As often as not these will be general
wet or dry flies. He casts and casts and casts. And, if he catches
a few trout he is pleased with himself.

Eventually our novice irons out problems in his casting. He
gains experience of his river beats and where the best trout lies
are. He learns which artificial flies give better results: but often
does not know why! He now manages to catch trout with some
consistency, especially early in the season when the year's stockies are still naive. He might even boast of big catches ("seventeen
in an afternoon!") but fails to point out, sometimes even to himself, that these were suicidal creatures fresh from the fish farm.
Still he will be able to hold his own amongst a large proportion
of trout anglers who never proceed further.

Sooner or later, alas, he will experience a blank day when,
despite his growing experience and technical ability with the
fly rod, the fish are obviously feeding but will not look at his
chosen flies. His response to such a sad day can be a milestone
in his progress as an angler. He can pack up in despair and go

PLATE 1

UPWINGED FLY

Ephemerid Dun. Notice
colouration and opaque wings.

OLIVE SPINNER

Note brighter appearance
and transparent wings.

EPHEMERID NYMPH

STONEFLY NYMPH

(2 tails)

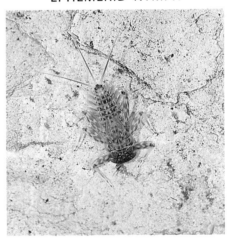

(3 tails) Ephemerid

Nymphs of both Stonefly and Ephemerid Flies are best imitated by a Sawyer's Pheasant Tail Nymph of
appropriate size or by a suitable Northern Hackled Wetfly.

Note: colour plates 1, 2 and 3 show varying magnifications from life size.

PLATE 2

ADULT SEDGE (Caddis)

ADULT MIDGE

BLOOD WORM LARVA

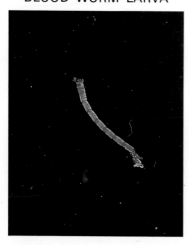

DIVING BEETLE LARVA

Two aquatic insect larvae of different structure and appearance.

home, a failure. He might go through the entire contents of his fly boxes in the hope that the fish may find one to their liking (more often than not when he does this one idiotic trout will be caught and "save the day"). The third alternative is that our angler will look at the river and work out, or attempt to work out exactly what the fish are feeding on. This might prove difficult. With the fish feeding keenly, the normal response of the angler is to hammer away with his flies; and the more he does this the more oblivious he becomes to everything but the fish and his determination to catch them. Certainly he will not feel like putting his rod aside to do a little paddling and nature study! But that is what he must do so that he can find and look at the natural fly that the trout are taking exclusively and say "Next time you are around, I will be prepared!" And then he can either tie for himself or purchase a suitable imitative pattern.

Unfortunately many never make this simple stride. They lack an inquisitive enquiring mind and are content to hammer away at the fish with flies that will patently not do. Such anglers miss out on the greatest pleasure that trout fishing has to offer. To see a fish feed. To identify the food. To devise or obtain a suitable imitation. To fool the fish into taking that imitation. Such is the triumph of the real fly-fisher.

To reach this position the angler must come to grips with natural foods of river trout.

There have been several texts published that deal specifically with the natural foods of trout and with aquatic and riverside animals and plants. It is not my aim to repeat them here. All trout anglers should have copies of John Goddard's *Trout Fly Recognition* (1976 3rd Ed.) and J. R. Harris's *An Angler's Entomology* (1956 Ed.) These are super references. Then there are the outstanding keys for the identification of freshwater animals and plants, produced by the Freshwater Biological Association at Windermere. Finally, there are a series of books that deal with the natural history of freshwaters. Of these I would recommend T. T. Macan and E. B. Worthington *Life in Lakes and Rivers* (1972 Ed.).

However this book deals with fishing for trout: mostly with fly. And as the angler's fly is, in theory at least, an imitation of a natural creature it would seem only logical to look at the

45

range of natural foods available to trout.

Apart from minnows and other small fish, including young trout, the bulk of the diet of river trout is composed of invertebrates. For non-biologist trout anglers a stumbling block exists that can hinder their development as anglers, and which if it can be overcome, results in an enhancement of pleasure and interest in their sport. That stumbling block is the apparent complexity of the types of fly and other invertebrates which comprise the food of trout and which the imitative fly represents. I can understand the problem. The bewildering number of names, both scientific and English. The complex but subtle features by which different groups are separated, one from the other. The complex nature of the insect life cycle. These can all puzzle and confuse the non-biologist; and even the biologist when he first encounters them.

Well I remember, when I first looked seriously at freshwater invertebrates, the problem I faced of having to absorb the names and identifying characteristics of so many small organisms. I was fortunate. As an undergraduate I spent a long term under the guidance of Dr. T. T. Macan, the foremost authority on freshwater animals. He would rattle off the names of invertebrates that we had collected and describe in detail their life-styles: they were common parlance to him. They were a new language to me and my fellow students. We would make our own collections from the lakes and streams of Cumbria and then, back in the laboratory, laboriously struggle through the keys to identify them. Macan simply glanced at a specimen: "Ah! Yes, *Ecdyonurus venosus*. A major ephemerid of the rocky streams of Northern England !". It was alright for him. He had spent a lifetime with these animals. We were using keys he had invented. We had been thrown in at the deep-end! And yet we had a lot of biological knowledge behind us. What chance would a non-biologist trout angler have?

Well the answer is a good chance! Provided crawling precedes walking, walking precedes running. In this chapter I will help you to crawl, start you walking and give you some guidance on how to run on the journey through the range of trout foods. I will chatter about invertebrates in general and deal with the major groups. Make sure you understand that first, and already you will have accumulated enough to benefit you by the river. Then we will deal with some species in this chapter and many others in the remaining chapters: we will be walking one step at a time. The running comes later.

Freshwater Invertebrates

Invertebrates are animals without backbones. So far, so good? And as biologists split vertebrates into different groups (mammals, birds, amphibians, reptiles and, thank goodness fish!) so invertebrates are separated into groups, the members of which have common features.

So, here we go; some examples of the major groups of invertebrates or "phyla".

Phylum (or group)

Protozoa: these are single-celled, microscopic animals (e.g. Amoeba)

Phylum Annelida: segmented worms (e.g. earthworms, lug worm)

Phylum Mollusca: the "molluscs" (e.g. snail, mussel, oyster)

Phylum Arthropoda: the main phylum as far as trout anglers are concerned and the one that I shall concentrate on.

Arthropoda means

Arthro = jointed (arthritis: inflamation of the joints in humans)

—*poda* = legs (tripod: three legs)

Arthropods then have jointed legs; or at least most of them have. Midge larvae lack legs; that is an exception. But adult midges have jointed legs.

The jointed nature of the legs and, for that matter the jointed or segmented nature of the entire arthropod body is a consequence of the arthropod skeleton. Vertebrates (such as you) have internal skeletons made of bone to which the muscles attach to allow for support and movement of the body. Arthropods have an external skeleton, sometimes wrongly called a "shell", made of a hard waxy material called "chitin" or mineral salts (e.g. lob-

47

ster and crab). This external skeleton must have joints if the animal is to move. Joints somewhat after the fashion of suits of armour worn by knights in medieval days: the rigid metal plates had leather joints. Indeed the old Sir Lancelot might have been classified as an arthropod if an extra-terrestrial biologist had found him in his suit of armour!

But there are many problems associated with having a rigid external skeleton. The most important problem common to all arthropods is that with a rigid skeleton the arthropod cannot grow. At least it cannot grow in its skeleton!

So, just as we, as children, throw away our shoes when our feet are becoming cramped and choose a larger pair, so does an arthropod. When it has outgrown its exoskeleton it simply casts it aside (it literally bursts at the seams) and then, in a short time, it grows a new one. But whilst the new one is developing and hardening it makes itself as big as it can so that it has room to grow inside its new suit! The shedding of the old and development of the new exoskeleton is known as moulting or, to biologists, as "ecdysis". Such is common to all arthropods.

Within the phylum Arthropoda are sub-groups known as "classes". Again the members within a given class have characters that are common to them all:

Phylum Arthropoda

Class Myriapoda (=myriads of feet): centipedes and millipedes
Class Crustacea: shrimps, crabs, lobsters and other crustaceans
Class Arachnida: mites, spiders and scorpions
Class Insecta: the insects
Only two of these classes have any real relevance to the trout angler: the crustaceans and insects.

Crustaceans

Freshwater crustaceans are easy to deal with in the context of river trout fishing because there are only three sizeable species in rivers. The first is the large (up to 10 centimeters long) crayfish that resembles a small lobster. Crayfish occur only in the cleanest alkaline rivers and streams. During the day they hide under boulders or holes in the river bank, and at night scavenge over the river bed for dead animal material or prey on tiny fish or other invertebrates. Big trout are quite fond of crayfish and I have frequently found, in the Wharfe, Aire and upper Ribble, the remains of crayfish in the stomachs of trout. However, this crustacean is not usually imitated by fly fishers though I suppose that one of the larger salmon prawn or shrimp "flies" might deceive a trout that is hooked on crayfish! But that might be considered not truly within the spirit of trout "fly-fishing".

The two smaller common river crustaceans are the water hog-louse (*Asellus*) and freshwater shrimp (*Gammarus*). These are especially abundant in slower, chalky, alkaline rivers with good weed growth, where they graze on detritus and algae from the weed shoots and amongst the weed roots. Both are important trout foods where they occur; and there are some excellent leaded imitations. Possibly the best of these is the Killer Bug, a pattern devised by the great nymph angler, the late Frank Sawyer. This should be cast to fish that are grubbing about for food on the river bed or taking food items from weed beds, possibly using the induced-take method (see chapter 5).

Freshwater crustaceans

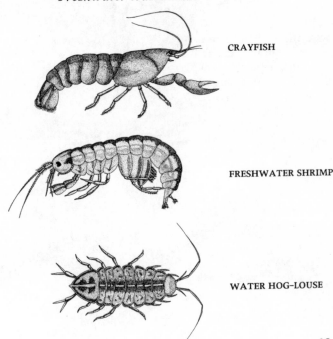

CRAYFISH

FRESHWATER SHRIMP

WATER HOG-LOUSE

A Range of Adult Insects

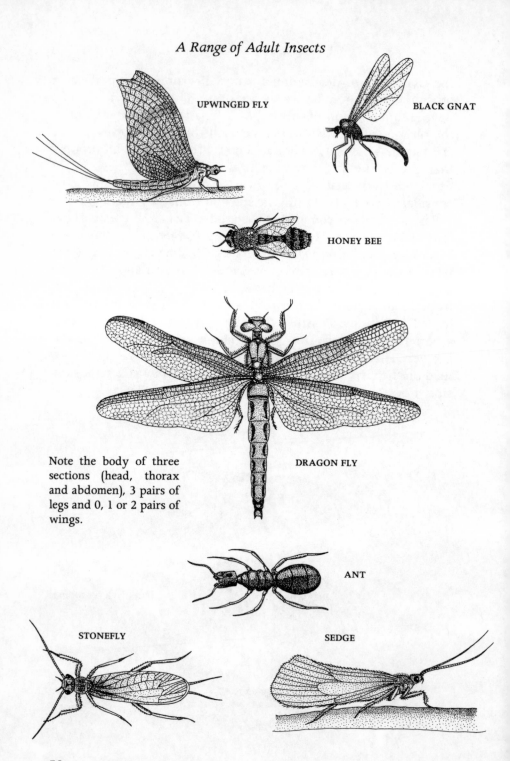

UPWINGED FLY

BLACK GNAT

HONEY BEE

DRAGON FLY

Note the body of three sections (head, thorax and abdomen), 3 pairs of legs and 0, 1 or 2 pairs of wings.

ANT

STONEFLY

SEDGE

Insects

Insects, as far as the trout angler is concerned, are very easy to identify. A cursory examination shows immediately three major body sections: head, thorax and abdomen. Often the head has antennae. The thorax almost always (fly maggots and midge larvae and pupae being exceptions) has three pairs of jointed legs and, in the flying adult stages, either one or two pairs of wings. In some insects the tip of the abdomen bears two or three filaments, in others the abdomen appears, from a quick glance, to lack any appendage. I would strongly recommend the novice to trout fishing, or the experienced trout angler who wishes to look at natural trout foods for the first time, to take a little time on the river bank, in the garden at home or wherever looking closely at as wide a range of insects as possible. Then they will become familiar with the features of insects that I have described above.

For the river trout angler four groups of insects are important though species from several other insect groups may occur at some time during the season on some rivers. Initially, however, I recommend the angler generally to ignore the latter and concentrate on the main four:

Ephemeroptera: the dayflies, upwinged flies or "may flies"
Examples: spring olive, march brown

Trichoptera: sedge flies or caddis flies
Examples: cinnamon sedge, silver horns

Plecoptera: stone.flies
Examples: willow fly, yellow sally

Diptera: two winged flies
Examples: housefly, midges, daddy-long-legs, gnats

Of the groups of lesser importance I suppose that overall the following four groups are most likely to be encountered by the river angler. It really should be possible to pick up the members of these groups easily.

Lepidoptera: moths. In warm summer evenings moths, crash-landing and spluttering across the surface of a slow pool, can provoke the trout to feed violently. At the same season caterpillars, descending on silk threads from trees overhang-

51

ing the water, can dominate the diet of trout in such lies.
(Normally these moth caterpillars descend to the earth
where they form pupae in the soil surface.)

Coleoptera: beetles. Though there are many species of aquatic
beetle they are of little importance to river trout anglers.
Not so in still waters where weed beds can have large beetle
populations. During population explosions that occur from
time to time, lots of land based beetles might find their way
into the river accidentally, blown from heather moors or
pastures, or fallen from trees overhanging the river.

Hemiptera: bugs (!). Pond skaters and water boatman are possibly the best known hemipterans to trout anglers but on
rivers they are insignificant as compared with their importance in some stillwater fisheries. But one type of hemipteran
can dominate the diet of river trout in September: the green
fly or aphis.

Hymenoptera: wasps and ants. It is the latter, in some summers, that might be swept in huge numbers by the wind
from the river bank vegetation and when this happens the
trout will feed on them to the exclusion, or so it appears,
of all others.

For each of these four groups the angler should be prepared
with one or two fly patterns. Tucked into a corner of the fly
box they might not be used in some years; but in many others
they will certainly save him from the ignominy of a blank day
when the fish are keenly feeding all around him!

For a trout angler really to come to grips with the insect food
of trout it is essential that the two basic contrasting styles of
the insect life cycle are understood. All insects go through a somewhat complicated life cycle, starting with the egg stage and end-
ing with the sexually-mature adult. Such life cycles are referred
to as metamorphoses.

Incomplete metamorphosis
The type of life cycle found in the insect classes Plecoptera (stoneflies) and Ephemeroptera (upwinged flies).

The egg hatches into a tiny "nymph"—some anglers refer to
this as a larva or larvula—which is almost a tiny miniature of

A series of Aquatic Nymphs

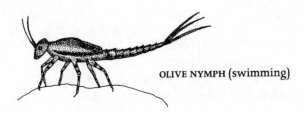

OLIVE NYMPH (swimming)

ECDYONURID (crawling)

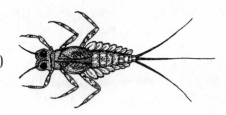

STONEFLY

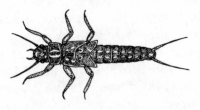

BURROWING (Mayfly)

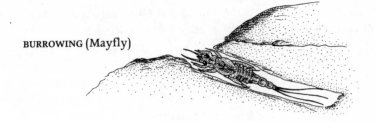

the parent though lacking wings and reproductive organs. The nymph feeds voraciously and, when necessary, stops feeding to moult its exoskeleton for a larger one. Thus it gains in size as it passes from one nymph stage to the next. Throughout its subaqueous existence breathing is carried out by gills which are easily visible in most species. In some species the gills are constantly in motion increasing the flow of oxygen-bearing water over them.

Stonefly nymphs, which occur in only the cleanest of rivers, dwell under boulders or amongst the gravel of the river bed. The nymphs of the upwinged flies can occur in a wide range of niches within the river, each species having its own to which it is specially adapted. The nymphs of the largest species, the mayfly, live in burrows that they construct with their huge mandibles. Those of the "angler's curse" or *Caenis* feed in the surface layers of mud and silt of the bed of slower pools. Two species of nymphs, one of which hatches into the famous blue winged olive, live amongst moss and stones on the river bed or in masses of decaying vegetation trapped between boulders or tree roots. Another group of nymph species are specially adapted for living in the fastest stony rivers, their streamlined flattened bodies and long sturdy legs enabling them to cling to the surface of boulders even in the strongest of currents. These comprise the family of upwinged flies known, to the scientist, as the ecdyonurids: a group of insects especially important to the anglers on upland streams in northern and western Britain. Finally there is a large series of upwinged fly nymphs that can swim. These include the nymphs of the pale wateries and olives. Some authors have separated these into two: the "laboured swimmers" and the "agile darters". They live in beds of river moss or weed and swim, rather than crawl, as a means of progression. Sketches of these different types are shown.

Eventually, at the appropriate season of the year, the nymph attains its full size. It then moults into a winged form. Here the pattern of metamorphosis in the stoneflies and upwinged flies diverges somewhat.

The fully-grown stonefly nymph emerges from the river bed, usually in the hours of darkness, by crawling out onto riverside boulders or vegetation. Here the final moult occurs to reveal the sexually mature adult or imago. In most species both sexes have wings and can fly. They crawl or fly into riverside bushes and trees which provide them with shelter from the elements and predators. Mating occurs and the female returns to the water where she deposits her fertilised eggs.

Life cycle of the Stonefly (Plecoptera)

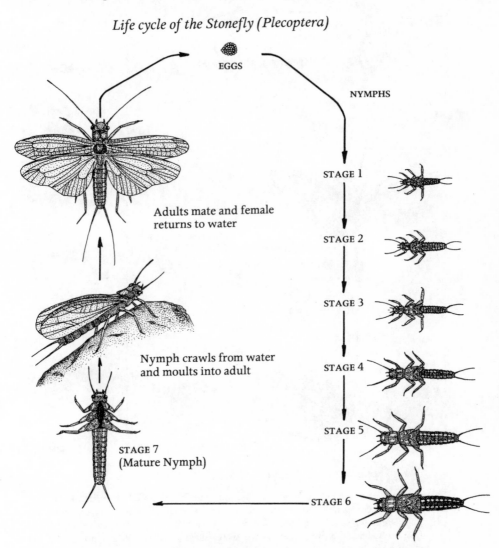

EGGS

NYMPHS

Adults mate and female returns to water

STAGE 1

STAGE 2

STAGE 3

Nymph crawls from water and moults into adult

STAGE 4

STAGE 5

STAGE 7
(Mature Nymph)

STAGE 6

The nymphs of stoneflies are important trout foods. However when trout are grubbing in the stream bed and taking these they are rarely, if ever, being selective and any leaded nymph or wet fly, properly fished, will suffice. The mature nymph crawls from the water to hatch into the adult and very few adults end up on the water after egg laying. So there is never the need for the angler to have imitations of stonefly adults (see text, page 117).

Life cycle of the Upwinged Fly (Ephemeroptera)

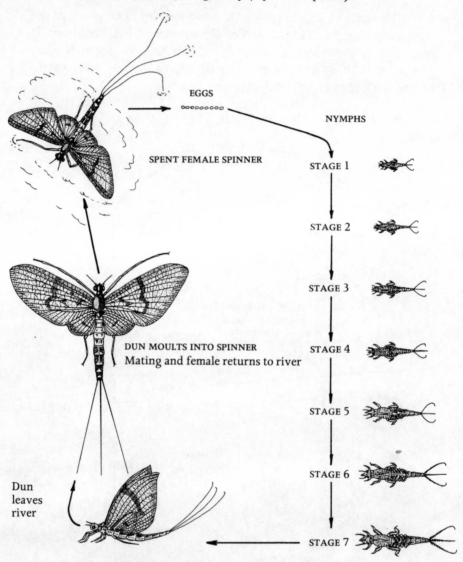

EGGS

NYMPHS

SPENT FEMALE SPINNER

STAGE 1

STAGE 2

STAGE 3

DUN MOULTS INTO SPINNER
Mating and female returns to river

STAGE 4

STAGE 5

Dun
leaves
river

STAGE 6

STAGE 7

ADULT EMERGES AS DUN

The upwinged flies have long been considered the major group of trout flies as far as the angler is concerned. Trout take the nymphs keenly, but are rarely selective when they are doing so. A suitable leaded nymph or wet fly will suffice, fished properly. In most species the duns hatch at the water surface when good imitations are needed; in a few the mature nymph crawls from the water and the trout rarely see the duns. After laying their eggs the female spinners are often taken by the trout; for these too the angler needs a reasonable imitation.

In the upwinged flies there are two flying stages. First of all there is the dun stage (so called because of the generally drab colouration) which emerges by moulting from the last nymph stage. In some species (notably the false march brown) the nymph crawls from the river, in the same manner as the stonefly, and moults to the dun on a riverside boulder or grass stem. In most (mayfly, true march brown, spring olive etc.) the fully grown nymph floats from the river bed to the water surface film. Quickly the nymphal exoskeleton (or shuck) splits and out pops the dun. The wings rapidly enlarge and, when dry, they are used to carry the dun from the water surface to the safety of riverside vegetation.

The time taken for the emergence of the dun from the nymph may last so long that where parts of the stream have a particularly fast flow the emerging dun may become waterlogged and drowned. Thus, during a hatch of duns, suitable wet fly patterns score heavily in weir pools and the broken water at the necks of boulder-strewn pools. Also, on damp or muggy days the wings of the newly hatched duns take longer to dry out. Thus they spend longer on the water surface and provide more attraction to the fish.

The duns of most species rest hidden away in nooks and crannies for up to two or three days depending on weather conditions. The cooler the weather, the longer the dun stage generally. But in one group of ephemeropterans, the angler's-curse or *Caenis*, the dun hatches almost immediately into the next stage: the spinner.

Most anglers rarely have opportunity for watching insects moult. Yet the dun to spinner moult is easy to observe. Carefully catch a dun (do *not* hold it by the wings) and place it into a jam jar which contains some crumpled newspaper. The newspaper provides firm footing for the new pet and, at the same time, absorbs surplus moisture from the air. Ensure an adequate air supply. So far, kids' stuff!

Take the dun(s) home and put them into the refrigerator. Then, after a couple of days, remove them to a warm room and watch. Before your very eyes will occur the transition from drab dun to bright sparkling spinner. And by doing this with a wide range of ephemerids you will become very familiar with both duns and spinners. If you tie your own flies then you have captive models to work from: the pleasure of devising a fly of your own that really works. Then, by using the later chapters in this book, or by referring to those recommended in the References given earlier in this chapter, you will be able to identify it to species. Trout fly fishing will then have become an inquisitive art rather than a mechanical pastime.

So, from the opaque-winged drab dun there emerges the sexually mature spinner. Spinners have usually a richly coloured translucent body: mahogany reds, ambers and creams. In the rays of the sun they often seem to gleam. Their wings are a gauzy transparent.

The spinners leave their hiding-hole, where they have roosted following their emergence from the dun stage, and form swarms where mating occurs. Whilst the mating-flight or "dance" varies in its choreography from one species to another, the basic pattern is common to all. The males fly to and fro, up and down in groups, almost as though each was trying to outdo the other and make himself the most desirable. The females join the swarms, choose a mate, and copulation, where sperm are passed from male to female, occurs on the wing. Once his job is done, the male falls, exhausted and spent. Mating frequently occurs away from the river, over fields, amongst trees and often, on sunny days, above the tarmac roads which absorb heat quickly and produce warm thermals which facilitate the mating dance. Thus few male spinners ever fall into the river and trout rarely take them.

The female spinner, however, flies back to the river where she lays her cargo of eggs. In most ephemeropterans the eggs are laid, a few at a time, by the female flying upstream and occasionally dipping the tip of her abdomen into the water where the eggs are released. In the blue winged olive the performance is similar except that the eggs are released in a single large mass. In a few species the eggs are attached to solid substrates by the female either actually crawing underwater (as in many *Baetis* species of olives) or crawling to the water's edge, backwards, and dipping her abdomen into the water.

Once all the eggs are laid the female spinner dies, often falling onto the river water surface. It is then called a spent spinner. Unlike duns, which stand proud on the water surface film, these dead and dying spinners lie flat and waterlogged in the flow where they can be very difficult to see. It is often a useful ruse, when the trout are feeding at the surface on you know not what, to try a spinner pattern. Analysis of the guts of trout caught in such circumstances usually reveals how correct was the choice of fly.

Complete Metamorphosis

This type of life cycle is familiar to most people who probably met it first, as small children, when they kept cabbage white butterflies: eggs hatch into larvae, larvae turn into pupae (or chrysalises), and from the pupae emerges the adult fly. For the coarse angler the dipteran cycle is well known. The maggot-breeder raises the maggots from the egg stage. The maggots, as in all dipterans, lack legs and other appendages. Then the maggots turn to pupae: the casters. Finally, from the caster emerges the blue-bottle adult; usually in the boot of the car!

In all dipterans the larvae resemble maggots (e.g. the leather jacket larva of the daddy-long-legs) or, in the case of most aquatic dipteran larvae (e.g. the buzzer-larvae of chironomids) resemble small grey, green or red segmented worms. The latter, though less well-known, can easily be observed if a handful of water-moss, weed or silt, collected from the bed of the slower pools, is put into a jam jar of clean water. Tiny writhing larvae are almost certain to be present.

Whilst most dipteran pupae resemble the butterfly chrysalises and blue-bottle caster, some aquatic dipterans have pupae that can maintain their position in the water by swimming. Mosquitoes and chironomids have such pupae that can swim. In these pupae again there are no real appendages, but a careful examination with a magnifying glass or microscope shows clearly, underneath the pupal exoskeleton, the outline of the adult features: wings, legs, antennae etc.

Most dipterans are land flies. Thus their larvae and pupae never appear in the river unless washed there by floods or thrown there by anglers. However any adult dipteran might occur on or in the river. Of course, those fewer species with earlier aquatic stages will occur, as do the duns of upwinged flies,

59

during a hatch. And as the spent female spinners of upwinged flies often fall onto the river after egg-laying so do the female dipterans after they have ovulated on the water surface. But the majority of species of dipterans are land-bred and it is only during windy conditions that these adults may be drifted onto the water. These "falls" are often seasonal, coinciding with the peak periods of activity of the adult flies: hawthorn flies and black gnats in May, dung flies in hot summer weather, daddy-long-legs in late summer.

Adult dipterans are often well-known: to be sure of the identity check the wings. There are two wings, one on either side of the thorax. But behind these can often be seen a tiny vestigial remnant wing known as a "halter" which resembles a miniscule drumstick. The abdomen lacks appendages; the head has large eyes and usually very tiny antennae.

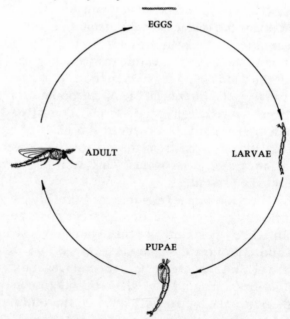

Life cycle of Diptera (Midge shown here)

Though trout feed on the larvae of aquatic Diptera they are difficult for the trout angler to imitate reasonably. The pupae, especially during a hatch, are easier to imitate as are also the adults. The adults of many land-bred Diptera often fall onto the water in large numbers (e.g. daddy-long-legs, hawthorn fly, dung fly) and these can be very important to both trout and angler.

PLATE 3

CORIXA

FRESHWATER SHRIMP

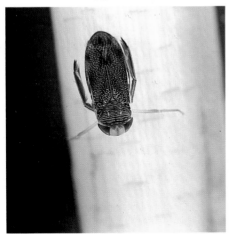 

Two common trout foods. The small water boatman or *Corixa* and the fresh-water shrimp or *gammarus*. When trout are feeding on these they tend not to be selective.

HATCHING DAMSEL

Ecdysis or moulting is essential for their growth. Here an adult damsel-fly emerges from its last nymphal stage.

PLATE 4

The upper Lune in the dog-days of summer. Bright sunlight, clear very low water and few hatches of fly in the day make trout fishing very difficult. Come dusk, however, with hatches of duns and sedge and falls of spinners, and the trout appear as if by magic!

Spring fish on a grassy bank.

Trichoptera: (the fourth major group of trout flies)

Sedges also progress through the same form of metamorphosis. Their eggs are laid on or in the water and the larvae, or caddis, in most cases build themselves a protective tube or case of sand, pebbles, bits of twig or leaf. The form of case is often characteristic to one particular species. In a few river species there is no case, the larvae dwelling amongst river moss which grows on boulders in the pools. There they form a tent like shelter using self-made silk as guy-ropes and the same material as a net, placed at the entrance to their lair, which collects food particles from the flow.

The caddis larvae blocks the openings of its case or lair prior to pupation and in this enclosure enters the pupal stage. From this haven the sedge or caddis fly either crawls ashore (as in the manner of the stoneflies) or floats to the water surface (as in the manner of the ephemerids).

Adult sedges can be difficult for the novice to identify, as superficially they closely resemble moths. They vary tremendously in size and colouration. Some less than a centimetre long, others three centimetres or more in length. Some are almost black, others the palest of buff. All sedges have four wings which are covered in tiny hairs (Trichoptera = hairy wing) as distinct from moths which have scales on their wings (Lepidoptera = scale wings). They have characteristically long, sometimes super-long antennae. At rest the wings of sedges are held, in tent fashion, over the body whereas in moths the wings are held flat over the body.

In the British Isles there are:
    34 recorded species of Stoneflies (Plectoptera)
    47 recorded species of upwinged flies (Ephemeroptera)
    190 recorded species of sedge (caddis) flies (Trichoptera) and
        hundreds of species of two-winged flies (Diptera)

There are also similarly large numbers of other insects (e.g. moths, alderflies, beetles, hymenoptera, etc.) as well as representatives of other invertebrate groups such as earthworms, slugs and snails that might occur on or in the water.

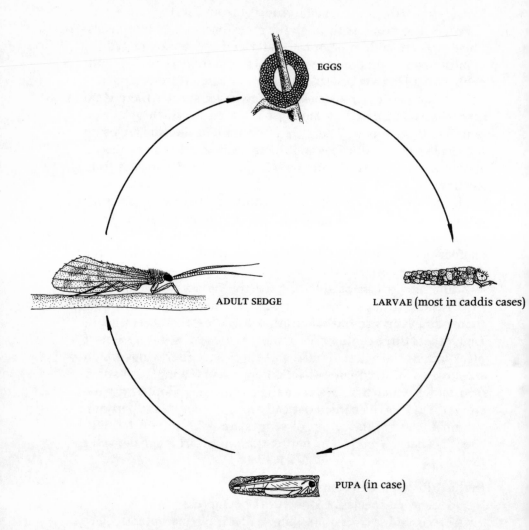

EGGS

ADULT SEDGE

LARVAE (most in caddis cases)

PUPA (in case)

Life cycle of Sedge or Caddis-fly (Trichoptera)

Though trout frequently take caddis from the river bed it is impractical for the angler to attempt to imitate these. In any case, grubbing trout are rarely selective feeders and any weighted nymph will catch them (see text). It is the adult sedge that, on a warm summer evening, the angler must prepare for with adequate dry fly or suitable wet fly.

62

Obviously some species will be more important than others to both trout and angler. These are the ones that I will highlight in future chapters; the ones that the newcomer to imitative river trout fishing must come to grips with as soon as possible.

The scientific keys such as those produced by the Freshwater Biological Association, deal with them all. Likewise the sort of text that I referred to earlier in the chapter (such as Goddard's *Trout Fly Recognition*) deals with most species. Such detail is not necessary for the trout angler, however, at least in the early stages of his development. Later, an obsessive amateur entomologist-cum-trout fisherman will have these as his bibles. But, in my opinion the extra detail that such references provide is not essential. So many species within one group are so similar that the trout angler may treat them as one; as does, I am sure, the feeding trout. Do the trout really distinguish between *Centroptilum luteolum, Centroptilum pennulatum, Procloeon bifidum*, and *Baetis fuscatus*? No! Neither need anglers for they are all basically "pale-wateries"!

So in later chapters we will deal with trout foods from the trout's point-of-view and the angler's point-of-view, not the stand point of the entomologist nor even the angler-entomologist.

CHAPTER FOUR

Trout Flies: Essential and Useful

Oft I have seen a skilful angler try
The various colours of the treacherous fly;
When he with fruitless pain hath skimmed the brook,
And the coy fish rejects the skipping hook,
He shakes the boughs that on the margin grow,
Which o'er the stream a waving forest throw;
When, if an insect fall (his certain guide),
He gently takes him from the whirling tide;
Examines well his form, with curious eyes,
His gaudy vest, his wings, his horn and size.
Then round his hook the chosen fur he winds
And on the back a speckled feather binds.

John Gay. 1720. *Poems on several occasions, containing*
Rural Sports.

In the following chapters I have referred to fly patterns that have proved themselves as successfully representing particular trout foods. Or, to put it another way, the trout will take them when feeding on certain specific food items. This chapter collects all the patterns together and provides details of the dressing for each. With such a selection of artificial flies I would be quite happy to face any feeding trout in any river or stream in the British Isles. The collection (which are shown on plates 5, 6, 7) includes some very popular traditional or well-established flies as well as some that are less well known.

For those who buy ready-dressed flies let me say this.

Make sure that you are getting the best. And the best are usually the most expensive. Check the hook quality. Give the hackle, tail and wings a little tug: they should not fall out when you do this. In dry flies check that the hackles are stiff: when the fly is stood on a table the hackles should bend a little but the fly should be still held proud and upright. In wet flies the dressing should be extremely sparse. If there are wings they should be narrow slips. The hackle should be no more than two turns. In weighted nymphs or bugs the fly should sink quickly: drop one into a cup of water. If it doesn't go "plop" and dive straight to the bottom, reject it. Check for correctness of dressing: many shop bought flies are ridiculous in that they bear no relationship to the true dressing. Finally, some patterns of fly will not be available "over-the-counter". If that is the case, have them made up for you by a good fly-tyer, either a friend or a professional.

Aire Mayfly Dun

Hook: Size 8. Mayfly.
Silk: Black.
Tail: Three fibres from cock pheasant tail.
Body: Natural raffene ribbed black and red silk.
Hackle: Blue dun cock with two turns of mallard drake breast feather dyed hot orange.

Aire Mayfly Spinner

Hook: Size 8. Mayfly.
Silk: Black.
Tail: Three fibres from cock pheasant tail.
Body: Natural raffene ribbed black silk.
Hackle: Blue dun cock.
Wings: Blue dun hackle points tied spent.

Ants

Hook: Size 14–16. Dry fly.
Silk: Orange or black.
Body: Tying silk wound round the hook to produce a large abdomen, narrow waist and large thorax.
Hackle: Natural red or black cock.
Wings: Pale blue dun hackle points, tied back.

65

Autumn Specials

These three flies, normally regarded as grayling flies, are excellent trout catchers in September. All are tied on size 14 hooks and can be dressed for dry fly or wet fly fishing by using appropriate hooks and cock or hen hackle.

1. Red Tag

Tag: Red wool.
Body: Peacock herl.
Hackle: Natural red.

2. Treacle Parkin

Tag: Yellow wool.
Body: Peacock herl.
Hackle: Natural red.

3. Sturdy's Fancy

Tag: Red wool.
Body: Peacock herl.
Hackle: Blue dun.

Beetles

1. Coch-y-Bonddu

Hook: Sizes 12–14. Dry fly.
Body: Peacock herl with a tag of gold tinsel.
Hackle: Coch-y-bonddu.

2. Cork Beetles

Hook: Sizes 10–14.
Body: Cork cut and shaped to size and tied onto the hook with silk. The whole is varnished twice and then painted to represent the required beetle. For example one can produce a "ladybird" by this means.
Hackle: Two turns of appropriately coloured hackle at the head end to represent the beetle legs.

Black Palmered Sedge

Hook :	Sizes 8–14. Dry fly or, for larger sedges, Mayfly.
Silk :	Black.
Body :	Black seal's fur.
Rib :	Fine silver wire.
Body hackle :	Black cock, palmered.
Shoulder hackle :	Black cock.

A good fly to try at night when sedges are on the water. Also a useful "desperation" fly in the smaller sizes, especially when dark flies or beetles are the main trout food.

Black and Peacock Spider

Hook :	Sizes 8–14. Wet fly.
Silk :	Black.
Body :	Peacock herl ribbed fine silver wire.
Hackle :	Black hen; three turns.

A wet fly to imitate the drowned hawthorn fly, black gnat or any other dark fly.

Brown Moth

Hook :	Size 10. Dry fly.
Body :	Brown seal's fur.
Hackle :	Natural red.
Wings :	Brown duck quill, large.

Brown Palmered Sedge

Hook :	Sizes 8–14. Dry fly or, for larger sedges, Mayfly.
Silk :	Brown.
Body :	Brown seal's fur.
Body hackle :	Natural red cock.
Rib :	Fine gold wire.
Shoulder hackle :	Natural red cock.
Wing (optional) :	Speckled pale turkey.

Coachman

Hook: Sizes 10–12. Wet fly.
Silk: Black.
Body: Peacock herl.
Hackle: Black or natural red hen.
Wings: White, from slips of duck "satins".

A useful wet fly for night fishing which the fish might take for a sedge or moth.

Daddy-Long-Legs

Hook: Sizes 8–12. Mayfly
Silk: Brown.
Body: Three to five strands of herl from a cock pheasant tail feather, ribbed fine gold wire.
Legs: Eight, made by knotting herls from a cock pheasant tail feathers, tied splayed out.
Hackle: Blue dun cock.
Wings: Cree hackle points.

There are several species of daddy-long-legs (crane fly). Some are quite small, especially in moorland areas, so it is worth carrying a range of sizes.

Dark Watchet

Hook: Sizes 14–16. Wet fly.
Silks: Purple and orange.
Body: Tying silks, dubbed as finely as possible with mole fur, wound to produce a distinct ribbed effect. The silks should show through clearly as the sparse dubbing provides a mere halo or "fuzz" around the silk body.
Hackle: Jackdaw throat hackle, two turns at most. An underwing hackle from a waterhen could be used as an alternative.

A superb wet fly when iron blues are on the water.

Deerhair Sedge

Hook: Sizes 10–12. Mayfly.

Silk: Brown.

Body: Spun deer hair, trimmed to give a sedge shape or outline. Some fly-tyers add an underside of green seal's fur spun onto a length of tying silk, tied in at the tail and brought forward underneath the deer fur body, after trimming and tied in at the head. This does not seem essential as far as the river trout is concerned in the late evening.

Hackle: Cree cock.

This has the advantage that it will go on floating all day and all night, even after it has caught several fish.

Green Caterpillar

Hook: Sizes 10–12. Sedge Hook.

Silk: Green.

Body: Green seal's fur, ribbed fine gold wire.

Hackle: Blue dun cock tied palmer fashion down the body and clipped very short.

The body tied round the bend of the curved Sedge Hook, has a realistic curled caterpillar shape.

Greenfly Imitations

The following two flies, normally used in grayling fishing, are good patterns to use when the trout are taking greenfly from the water in late August and September.

Hook: Sizes 16–18. Silk Green.

1. Green Insect: Wet fly.

Tag: Red floss.

Body: Peacock herl from green sword feather.

Hackle: White hen.

2. Witch: Dry fly.

Tag: Red floss.

Body: Peacock herl from green sword feather.

Body hackle: White cock.

Head hackle: White cock.

Greenwell's Glory (Dry)—variants

Hooks:	Sizes 12–18. Dry fly.
Silk:	Primrose, yellow or olive well waxed.
Tail (optional):	Bunch of hackle fibres.
Body:	Tying silk ribbed fine gold wire.
Hackle:	Furness (Greenwell) cock.
Wings (optional):	Slips of starling or mallard quill, tied upright and split, or hackle points of blue dun.

See also suggestion on page 80, under Fly Tying Notes (3).

The Greenwell's Glory as used nowadays is really a range of flies based on different shades of tying silk and different hook sizes. In its darker and larger forms it is a good pattern to use when spring olives are on the water. In its paler and smaller forms it will take trout that are feeding on pale wateries. And in between it can be used to imitate the blue winged olive or, at a pinch any other ephemerid that might occur. One of the classics and still one of the best!

Greenwell's Glory (Wet)—variants

The tying is as the dry fly but with wet fly hooks, hen hackle and wings tied sloping back in true wet fly manner. By having a range it is possible to choose one with a size and colour tone to match what happens to be on the water. Tied without wings and with a very sparse hackle (two turns only) it makes an excellent unweighted nymph.

Grey Duster

Hook:	Sizes 14–22. Dry fly.
Silk:	Grey or brown.
Body:	Light rabbit fur dubbed on tying silk.
Hackle:	A well marked cock badger hackle.

One of the best patterns to use when the trout are preoccupied with small pale midges.

Hawthorn Fly

Hook: Sizes 12–14. Dry fly.
Silk: Black.
Abdomen: Black floss silk tied round the hook bend.
Rib: Peacock herl.
Thorax: Peacock herl, exaggerated.
Hackles: Black cock and natural red cock tied separately.

The best dry fly for hawthorn flies I have come across. Also a useful black gnat imitator.

Jacques' Blue Winged Olive

Hook: Size 14. Dry fly.
Silk: Orange.
Tail: Bunch of hackle fibres.
Body: Olive plastic sheet wound over a dirty yellow ostrich herl underbody.
Hackle: Light olive cock.
Wings: Two pairs from coot wing slips.

Kite's Imperial

Hook: Sizes 14–16. Dry fly.
Silk: Purple.
Tail: Bunch of hackle fibres.
Body: Ash grey heron herl, doubled and redoubled at the thorax, ribbed fine gold wire.
Hackle: Honey dun cock (dyed or natural).

One of the best dry flies to use when duns are on the water. If I was allowed only one dry fly pattern throughout the season I would choose the Imperial: in a wider range of sizes!

Malc's Special

Hook: Sizes 14–18. Dry fly.
Silk: Yellow.
Tail: Bunch of hackle fibres.
Body: Swan herl dyed yellow, doubled and redoubled at the thorax, ribbed fine gold wire.
Hackle: Golden olive cock (Fishermens Feathers).
Wings: Blue dun hackle points.

71

M.G. Green Dun

Hook: Sizes 14–16.
Silk: Green.
Tail: Bunch of hackle fibres.
Body: Swan herl dyed pale green, doubled and redoubled at the thorax, ribbed fine gold wire.
Hackle: Golden olive cock (Fishermens Feathers).
Wings (optional): Blue dun hackle points.

A good dun imitation especially when the dark dun, large green dun, olive upright and yellow dun are on the water.

M.G. Iron Blue Dun

Hook: Size 16. Dry fly.
Silk: Crimson.
Tail: Bunch of hackle fibres.
Body: Darkest blue heron herl ribbed with tying silk.
Hackle: Dyed iron blue cock (Fishermens Feathers).

M.G. Olive

Hook: Sizes 14–16. Dry fly.
Silk: Olive.
Tail: Bunch of hackle fibres.
Body: Swan herl dyed dull olive, doubled and redoubled at the thorax, ribbed fine gold wire.
Hackle: Golden olive cock (Fishermens Feathers).

An olive dun that the fish will take during hatches of the blue winged olive and small dark or medium olives.

M.G. Orange Spinner

Hook: Sizes 14–16. Dry fly.
Silk: Orange.
Tail: Bunch of hackle fibres.
Body: Swan herl dyed hot orange, ribbed fine gold wire.
Hackle: Blue dun cock.
Wings: Blue dun hackle points, tied spent.

A good pattern to try whenever ephemerid spinners are on the water.

Norris' Pale Watery Quill

Hook: Sizes 16. Dry fly.
Silk: Cream or primrose
Tail: Fibres from pale cream cock hackle.
Body: Stripped quill from cream hackle.
Hackle: Cream cock.
Wings: Teal secondary wing feather slips, tied upright and split.

Olive Spider

Hook: Sizes 14. Wet fly.
Silk: Olive
Body: Tying silk
Hackle: Olive hen, two turns at most

A wet fly that can be used to imitate the blue winged olive dun, other olives and as a general unweighted nymph pattern.

Orange Partridge

Hook: Size 14. Wet fly.
Silk: Orange.
Body: Tying silk ribbed fine gold wire.
Hackle: Brown partridge, two turns at most.

A fine general wet fly, especially useful in early spring or when blue winged olives are hatching.

Orange Quill

Hook: Sizes 14–16. Dry fly.
Silk: Orange.
Tail: Bunch of blue dun cock hackle fibres.
Body: Stripped white hackle stalk dyed hot orange.
Hackle: Blue dun cock.
Wings: Blue dun hackle points, tied spent.

A superb spinner pattern when fish are taking great red spinners, blue winged olive spinners etc.

73

Paythorne Caenis

Hook:	Sizes 18–22.
Silk:	Black.
Tail:	Bunch of hackle fires.
Abdomen:	Stripped white hackle stalk with one turn of silk showing at the tip.
Thorax:	Two turns of fine peacock herl.
Hackle:	Blue dun cock hackle.
Wings:	White hackle points, tied spent.

Peter Ross

Hook:	Sizes 8–12. Wet fly.
Silk:	Black
Tail:	Golden Pheasant tippets.
Body:	Rear half silver tinsel, front half dubbed red fur, the whole ribbed fine round tinsel.
Hackle:	Black hen.
Wings:	Barred teal flank feather slips.

Really a sea trout or loch trout fly, this can be used on rivers where its use is permitted to imitate tiny fish on which the larger trout are preying.

Pheasant Tail Spinner

Hook:	Sizes 14–16. Dry fly.
Silk:	Orange.
Tail:	Bunch of hackle fibres.
Body:	Ruddiest cock pheasant tail herls ribbed fine gold wire.
Hackle:	Natural red cock.

Poult Bloa

Hook:	Sizes 14–16. Wet fly.
Silk:	Yellow.
Body:	Tying silk.
Hackle:	Sooty grey feather from underwing of young red grouse.

A good standard wet fly which is especially good in size 14 when blue winged olives are hatching and size 16 when pale wateries are hatching.

Sawyer's Killer Bug

Hook: Sizes 10–16. Wet fly.
Silk: None: fine reddish copper wire is used.
Body: An underbody of wire is built up and then a strand of medium grey darning wool is tied in, wound over the underbody, and then tied off at the hook eye with the wire. The wool used by Sawyer is no longer made but a suitable alternative is available from haberdasher's shops.

An excellent "fly" when fish are grubbing for shrimps, water hog-louse and nymphs in the river bed.

Sawyer's Pheasant Tail Nymph

Hook: Sizes 14–16. Wet fly.
Silk: None. The finest copper wire is used.
Body: An underbody, with a pronounced thorax, is built up of wire. Three or four fibres from a cock pheasant tail are tied in by the tips so that the tips become very short nymph tails. The wire and pheasant herls are then twisted together into a rope which is wound up to the eye to make the body. The dark base to the pheasant herls are then passed back and forth over the thorax to produce an exaggerated thorax nymphal wing case.

The best of all nymph patterns.

Sedge Pupae

Hook: Sizes 10–12. Sedge Hooks.
Silk: Brown, orange or green as per abdomen colour.
Abdomen: Brown, orange or green seal's fur, ribbed fine gold wire.
Thorax: Ostrich herl dyed in the colour of the abdomen.
Hackle: Brown partridge, tied in rather long to represent wing cases, legs and folded antennae of the sedge adult.

A good bushy wet fly to use as the light fades and sedges are hatching. I tie them in a wide range of colours to use in still-waters; on rivers those given above have given the best results.

Silver March Brown

Hook: Sizes 10–12. Wet fly.
Silk: Orange.
Tail: Fibres from speckled partridge tail feather.
Body: Silver tinsel.
Hackle: Brown partridge.
Wings: Hen pheasant secondary wing quill slips tied sloping backwards.

An alternative to Peter Ross.

Snipe and Purple

Hook: Sizes 14–16. Wet fly.
Silk: Purple.
Body: Tying silk.
Hackle: Small feather from upper wing of snipe, two turns at most.

A good fly to use when trout are taking iron blue duns. It is also an excellent general wet fly.

Suspender Buzzer

Hook: Sizes 14–18. Wet fly or Sedge Hooks.
Silk: Orange, black or olive.
Float: Polystyrene bead enclosed in ladies' tights material.
Body: Orange, black or olive seal's fur ribbed fine gold lurex.
Thorax: Peacock herl.

These are good imitations of midge pupae, suspended beneath the surface film just before hatching. Taken from stillwater trout angling, where midges are important food items, they prove their worth in the slower river trout pools.

Titchy Midge

Hook: Sizes 18–26. Dry fly (Midge hooks).
Silk: Any colour you like: olive, orange and black are good to start with.

PLATE 5

DRY FLIES

MG Orange
Spinner

Orange Quill

Tup's Indispensable

Paythorne
Caenis

MG Green Dun

Jacques' BWO

MG Olive Dun
(with dark body)

MG Olive Dun
(with pale body)

Malc's Special
(winged)

Malc's Special
(hackle)

Norris' Pale
Watery Quill

Titchy Midge

Witch

Grey Duster

Wickham's Fancy

Coch-y-Bonddu

Olive Spider

Kite's Imperial

MG Iron Blue

Pheasant Tail
Spinner

Dry March
Brown

Greenwell's Glory
(spent wing dry)

Greenwell's Glory
(split wing dry)

Greenwell's Glory
(hackle dry)

PLATE 6

BUGS AND NYMPHS

Sawyer's Killer Bug   Suspender Pupa   Sawyer's Pheasant Tail Nymph   Green Caterpillar

LARGE WET FLIES

March Brown Nymph   Wet March Brown   Silver March Brown   Peter Ross

Sedge Pupa   Woodcock and Yellow   Coachman   Black and Peacock Spider

DRY FLIES

Black Ant   Hawthorn Fly   Red Ant

SMALL WET FLIES

Greenwell's Glory (wet winged)   Greenwell's Glory (wet spider)   Orange Partridge   Poult Bloa   Dark Watchet

Williams' Favourite   Waterhen Bloa   Green Insect   Yellow Partridge   Snipe and Purple

Body: Tying silk with clear thin polythene strips wound over.

Hackle: Blue dun or natural white cock.

Beware! Strike (tighten!) very late when using such tiny hooks for the fish take them slowly. And carefully! For such irons require very light leader points 1 lb B.S. or thereabouts.

Tup's Indispensable

Hook: Sizes 14–16. Dry fly.

Silk: Primrose.

Tail: Bunch of hackle fibres.

Body: Yellow floss silk with a tiny dubbing of creamy pink fur (tup's mixture) at the thorax.

Hackle: Honey dun cock.

An indispensable fly when pale wateries are about.

Waterhen Bloa

Hook: Sizes 14–16. Wet fly.

Silk: Yellow.

Body: Tying silk dubbed with mole's fur (50% natural and 50% dyed olive well mixed). The dubbing must be very sparse so that the silk shows clearly through.

Hackle: Underwing covert of waterhen; two turns only.

A good pattern to use when olives are hatching.

Wickham's Fancy (wingless)

Hook: Sizes 12–14. Dry fly.

Tail: Bunch of hackle fibres.

Body: Gold tinsel.

Body hackle: Natural red cock.

Rib: Fine gold wire.

Hackle: Natural red cock.

Usually Wickham's Fancy has wings (from starling): I have omitted them as they seem to serve no real purpose. It is a good fly when dung flies are being drifted onto the water; also when small sedges are on the river.

Williams's Favourite

Hook: Sizes 14–16. Wet fly.
Silk: Black.
Body: Tying silk ribbed fine round silver tinsel.
Hackle: Black hen, two turns only.

An excellent black wet fly.

Woodcock and Yellow

Hook: Sizes 8–10.
Silk: Yellow.
Tail: Golden pheasant tippets.
Body: Seal's fur ribbed fine gold wire.
Hackle: Natural red hen.
Wings: Slips from woodcock secondary quill.

An excellent big bushy wet fly for summer nights when sedges and moths are on the water.

Woolley's March Browns

Hook: Sizes 12–14. Tying silk orange.

1. Dry

Tail: Blue dun cock hackle fibres.
Body: Dubbed with well mixed yellow and brown fur, ribbed fine gold wire.
Hackle: Brown partridge and blue dun cock, well mixed.

2. Wet

Body: Sandy fur from hare's neck, ribbed yellow silk.
Hackle: Pale brown partridge.
Wings: Thin, speckled partridge tail.

3. Nymph

Tail: Three strands of brown mallard.
Body: Pheasant tail fibres with a thorax of dubbed brown fur and ribbed gold wire.
Hackle: One turn of speckled grouse hackle.
Wing cases: Fibres of woodcock feather.

Yellow Partridge

Hook: Sizes 14–16. Wet fly.
Silk: Yellow.
Body: Tying silk, ribbed fine gold wire.
Hackle: Grey partridge, two turns at most.

An excellent pale wet fly for summer when pale wateries are hatching.

Fly Tying Notes
Although the basics of fly tying are beyond the scope of this book I would like to make just a few points.

It is evident that river trout are never selectively fastidious feeders to the extent that they require in the artificial fly every little feature that is found in the natural fly. Thank goodness, or we would find life really hard! It seems rather that the trout look for certain triggers or foci on the natural fly and it is these that the imitative fly must match or exaggerate. Such foci may be one or several of the following:

1. Size—it is worthwhile tying many flies in a range of size so that if one is refused an alternative may be offered. Curiously artificial dry flies that are a little smaller than the natural fly are frequently more successful than ones of the same or a bigger size.

2. Wings—it is much simpler to tie flies without wings and often these are very effective. Thus many wet flies are of the spider-variety and, in recent years, an increasing number of dry flies have been of the wingless hackled variety. Sometimes, however, the trout will only take a winged fly. I would suggest, therefore, that the fly box should always contain several winged patterns.

    For dry fly wings the earlier tyers used slips from starling wing primary or secondary feathers. Most amateur fly-tyers find these very difficult because of their fragility and tendency for the fibres to separate. So can I pass on a tip given to me by Jack Norris: use slips from mallard or teal secondary quills until you get really familiar with tying the split wing. Though these are a little heavier than starling

79

the fibres are stronger and remain together much better. And the fish don't seem to mind the substitution. An alternative, that I use a lot, is to use hackle-point wings (buy a cheap blue dun cock cape for this purpose) or wings cut with a special wing-cutting tool.

3. Colouration—colour has dominated the fly-dresser throughout the history of fly-tying. In recent years the situation has become quite ridiculous: we have fluorescent materials, sparkle-yarn, flashabou, glitteryarn, doll body etc. etc. All materials, we are told, that are just about essential if we are going to catch trout. Such gaudy materials have some merits in producing flashy attractor reservoir lures. But in imitative fly-tying for river trout simplicity and subtlety of shade and colour are essential, often best provided by traditional silk, fur and feather.

No-one knows exactly what a trout sees as far as colours are concerned. Sometimes they seem almost oblivious to colour differences between artificial and natural flies: consider the efficiency of the Imperial, a fly that bears little resemblance to the flies it can be used to represent. Sometimes, however, the trout can demand quite a precise match of colour. It is thus worthwhile having a few standard patterns tied in a range of shades. For example, the Greenwell's Glory. Try tying them with silk bodies ranging from straw, through primrose and light yellow to yellow and olive (Pearsall's Gossamer Numbers 2–5 and 16), and with a range of hackle shade from light furnace (sometimes called Greenwell) to a very dark furnace. Sometimes the fish will take them all with gay abandon; on others they may select the darker tones and on others, the lighter ones.

4. Shape—the shape of the natural fly is often the last thing that the fly dresser thinks of including in his imitation. Yet, to the trout, this must be one of the most obvious features. Again, in some circumstances there is no real difficulty—the fish are not selective. But sometimes, when they are being a bit finicky, a little care in stressing a pronounced thorax or curved abdomen or segmented body can make the pattern more effective.

I believe that the thorax is one important "trigger" and that this is the big advantage of the "Netheravon Style" of herl-bodied dry flies promoted by Oliver Kite. At the thorax (i.e. just behind where the hackle will be tied later) the body of the fly is built-up by doubling and re-doubling the herls. It is well-worth attempting to produce a swollen thorax on the imitation wherever possible.

In some insects the abdomen is markedly curved: for examples midge pupae, sedge pupae, hawthorn fly. Again I suggest that including this in the artificial will improve the effectiveness of the fly. With a standard hook take the abdomen round the hook bend; a better alternative is to use the curved Grub or Sedge hooks that are on the market.

Segmentation is traditionally imitated by ribbing the body with fine tinsel or lurex, silk or fine wire, or by using a segmented body material such as quill or horse-hair.

5. No matter how superb the imitation, a major trigger or focus that the real fly always has and the artificial fly must be given, is a natural behaviour in or on the water. We must fish our fly so that its behaviour imitates the natural. And this leads us on to the next chapter.

CHAPTER 5

Styles of Fly Fishing

"... most flies are tied for up-stream fishing. That is to say they represent insects whose natural behaviour in the water is that of creatures incapable of resisting the current in any way. If these things are to be good deceivers, 'drag', even underwater 'drag' must be avoided. And 'drag' is the chief characteristic of the motion of flies describing wide arcs below the fisherman. . . ."

Arthur Ransome. *Rod and Line*. 1929

Three different styles of fly fishing fill the repertoire of the river angler: dry fly, wet fly and nymph. But a word of warning. On some beats of some rivers the rules restrict the angler to upstream dry fly only; or dry fly and nymph after a certain date, again cast upstream to feeding fish. Such rules must be adhered to even if the angler considers them nit-picking. For fishery rules are often made, not for the individual angler, but to maintain and protect the fishing for *all* anglers and the future. Every year a few fishermen break fishery rules and feel aggrieved that they are expelled from the club or syndicate, or are banned for life from a fishery. It serves them right. People who break rules do so in order to catch more fish "no matter what". To get one over on other anglers who obey the rules. To cheat the fishery owner. So double-check on fishing methods before you start and if the permit says "Dry Fly Only" then stick to the dry fly.

What a sad way to start a chapter! It might seem that this paragraph would not need saying. But it does! Some anglers, being human and tainted with 20th century competitive "civilisation" are greedy and their sole aim is to leave the water with as many fish in the bag as possible. And if necessary they will bend or ignore the rules to achieve their aim. How pathetic are such people! Angling is an art, employing the cunning of the hunter and inquisitiveness of the scientist. Angling, certainly for river trout with the fly, should require reasoning, problem solving, observation of the river and its environment. A fish in the bag is the culmination of all these facets.

The basic idea of fly fishing for river trout is to offer the trout an imitation of what it happens, at the time, to be feeding on. At its simplest the angler sees a fly floating downstream. The fly disappears in a swirl. Having identified the fly and chosen a suitable imitative pattern the angler casts his artificial fly so that it drifts downstream on the same path as the unfortunate natural. A swirl. The rod is raised. The fish is hooked and played out. It can be that easy, provided the angler has an artificial that fish will accept as a suitable imitation of what it is feeding on.

It is less simple when the fish are taking food that is beneath the water surface or in the surface film as the natural food is not easy to discern. In fact when they are feeding just under the water surface, possibly on nymphs, they may break the water surface and give the impression that they are taking from the surface. There is then the temptation, for the angler who prefers to fish the dry fly, to hammer away at them with a range of dry flies. A bit irrational this, especially when it is patently obvious that there are no natural flies floating on the surface!

A useful ploy, when this is happening or for that matter, whenever dry fly fails when fish are active at or close to the surface, is to put aside the rod for a few moments. Close examination of the flow might reveal a steady stream of the particular food item. Once, for instance, I went through the repertoire of dry flies (there were lots of midges and small olive duns on the water) and then discovered that the fish were actually taking the grey midge pupae that were drifting downstream just beneath the water film. Then, with a suitable nymph imitation success came rapidly. So common is this sort of event that I would recommend anglers to carry a tiny "pond net" with which they can effectively sample the river-borne potential food items.

The net which rolls up easily in the fishing bag, can be used to find out what is being carried downstream and therefore what the trout may be feeding on. The angler stands in the stream

83

downstream of the net with the cane supports held apart and the lower weighted end of the net beneath the surface. A quick look will then suggest the likely trout foods and a suitable imitative nymph or fly chosen.

A sampling net for the river angler

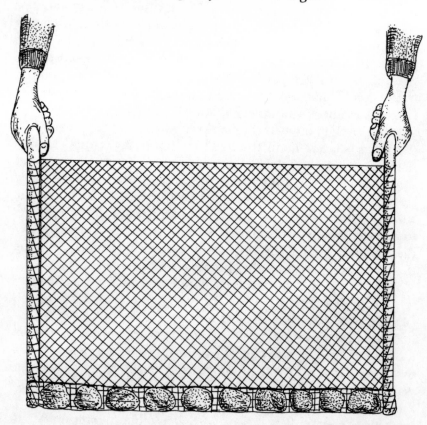

A length of fine-mesh net curtain is fixed to two garden canes, and a wide open hem left on the lower edge. Before use this hem has some pebbles from the river bank added to weight the net down. The net is then held, at an angle, against the current so that invertebrates wash into it. If you have a partner, have him hold the net and you rummage amongst water weed or boulders upstream of the net. You will then collect a representative sample of what is there available to the trout.

When not in use the net rolls up and is easily carried across the fishing bag.

It is much more difficult, on the face of it, to know what the fish are feeding on when they are active deep in the pools. However, when they are grubbing about in weed beds or amongst the gravel of the river bed they tend not to be fastidious and any *good* leaded nymph or bug pattern of appropriate size will often suffice. Indeed, the great nymph angler, the late Oliver Kite, used nothing else but Sawyer's Pheasant Tail Nymph. However, unless the river water is crystal-clear and the light direction and intensity good the problem here is that the trout cannot be seen. If such is the case then fishing must be by trial-and-error, the angler casting to where the fish are thought or likely to be lying.

In the depth dimension there are five zones in which the fish might find their food and in which the angler may catch his fish:

1) standing proud on the water surface film;
   This might include duns, land flies, midges and sedges. The method to employ is the simplest: DRY FLY

2) lying flat in the surface film;
   This might include duns that have been blown over, dead spent spinners, waterlogged dead land flies, greenfly, ants and caterpillars etc.
   The method to employ is again: DRY FLY. But in this case the dry fly ought to settle into the surface rather than float high on the surface.

3) just beneath the surface film;
   This might include drowned flies that have been washed under the surface, but often includes mature nymphs and the pupae of upwinged flies, midges and sedges that are near to hatching.
   The methods to employ are either standard wet flies (provided one may use them on that particular beat) or unweighted nymphs.

4) deep in the pool (for example amongst weed beds);
   This might include the nymphs of upwinged flies, shrimps, water hog-louse, and the larvae of some caddis and midges. The method to employ is either a heavy wired or leaded nymph or "bug" pattern.

5) from amongst detritus, gravel or boulders of the riverbed;
    This might include stonefly or upwinged fly nymphs, cad-
    dis larvae, shrimps and water hog louse.
    The method to employ is exactly the same as number 4. It
    is easy to devise a fly that will attach itself to the riverbed,
    but this is certain only to become snagged. Fish that are
    rooting for food actually in the riverbed are easily identified
    by their head down and tail up posture and the disturbed
    sediment produced by their labours. Invariably they take
    their food as it drifts downstream after being washed out
    by a combination of the disturbance caused by the fish and
    the flow. Fish which are rooting about in this manner can
    be seen swirling downstream to intercept such food items.
    Thus these foods can be represented, by the angler's leaded
    nymph or bug, exactly as are foods categorised in number
    4.

Should the fly be cast upstream, dowstream or across the flow?
Despite what some would have us believe it is possible to catch
trout on any type of fly in a river no matter whether one casts
it upstream, downstream or across the stream. The only clear-cut
rule is that to catch your fish the fly must be on or in the water.
And, of course, having stated the rule I must give the exception!
On a handful of occasions I have had the trout take a dry fly
in mid-air, just before the fly has alighted on the river surface.

Often I have taken trout (and grayling) by drifting a dry fly
down to them on a slack line: something not normally recommended. But when that is the only way to get the fly to the fish
drift it downstream you must! However, the most effective direction of cast is *almost* always upstream.

Consider the position of the feeding river trout. It faces
upstream so that it can collect food items that drift downstream
towards it. It faces upstream so that the water flows into its
mouth, through the gill filaments which absorb oxygen and
excrete carbon dioxide, and out via the gill cover. It faces
upstream so that it can hold its position in the water easily and
with the minimum expenditure of energy, utilizing its streamlined shape. Occasionally a trout will deviate sideways or downstream to intercept some morsel of food: but the prey will

invariably have been observed as it approached from upstream or as it passed the side of the trout's head.

Such being the case, that the trout will expect food to drift downstream towards it, why is it better to cast the artificial fly upstream?

The following are the advantages of casting upstream to feeding trout:

1. As the trout faces upstream so an angler casting downstream (i.e. from upstream of the fish) will be more visible to the fish, especially in clear low water conditions. Go and see for yourself. Find a feeding trout by creeping quietly upstream and searching the river with the aid of polaroid glasses. Then signal a friend to approach, again stealthily, from upstream. Have him wave his rod to and fro, mimicking casting. In nine out of ten such trials the fish will either dart off or show signs of unrest by increasing fin movements, dropping slightly back downstream or moving quietly into adjacent cover. A frightened fish is difficult to catch; one that has departed is impossible to catch.

So, a stealthy approach from downstream of the fish gives the best chance of having a catchable fish still in its lie.

2. When cast in a "down-and-across" style or even across the flow, as is often the accepted norm by some northern wet fly

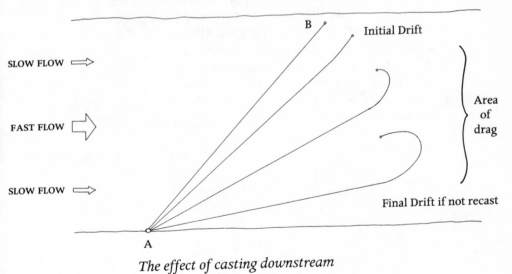

The effect of casting downstream

specialists, the fly or team of flies do not behave naturally. They either drift across the current or, by the angler retrieving line, advance upstream. And how many tiny nymphs, larvae, pupae or drowned duns (that the soft-hackled wet fly is meant to represent) can swim *against* fast water at speeds that prevent them being swept downstream rapidly? The answer is none. Consider the diagram on page 87.

The angler casts from A to B, the line falling across a band of fast water. The fly drifts initially as any slackness in the line is picked up by the current. Then a downstream belly forms in the line as the part of the line that lies in the faster flow is pulled down more rapidly than the farther end of the line, leader and flies. This belly pulls the flies quickly and unnaturally across the stream until eventually the leader and flies are on the angler's side of the fast flow. Then the flies will drift, more naturally, downstream until they eventually hang in the flow immediately below the angler.

Many fishermen who employ this technique may have noticed that a large proportion of the fish they catch are hooked soon after the flies have hit the water and that they have more offers if they cast as slack a line as possible, thereby increasing the duration of this initial drift. They may also have noticed that the second most productive part of the cast is during the last stage of the cast when again there is a period of natural drift. In some experiments, for every ten offers to the fly on the initial drift, no offers came during the period of drag and about four offers came in the later drift, as the cast was fished out. But whereas about 65% of offers that came in the initial drift were hooked and landed, less than 40% of offers in the last drift of the cast successfully resulted in fish in the net. I will refer back to this in a moment.

By casting upstream the line, leader and fly come downstream with the current and the debilitating effects of drag are greatly reduced. The fly is brought back towards the rod by the angler recovering line so that the fly drifts downstream at the same speed as the flow.

There is a problem in that, if one casts directly upstream so that the fly lands well upstream of the fish then it might be disturbed by the heavy fly line splashing onto the water. So if the

88

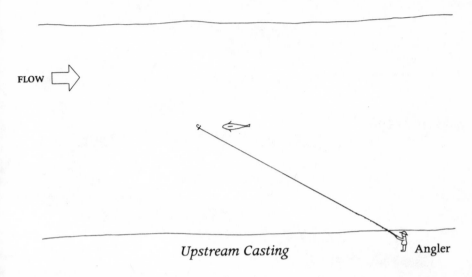

FLOW

Upstream Casting　　　　　　　　Angler

angler casts directly over the trout's lie then he must ensure that only the light leader falls over the fish.

In practice the cast is usually made "up-and-across" and thus disturbance caused by the line landing over the trout's lie will not occur. But remember. The more across-river the cast is made, the more the drag! It is a matter of trial-and-error. Of getting to know your rivers and trout lies intimately. Of gaining experience. Then comes the rule that so many anglers fail to observe. "Watch and think!" Watch the lie and flow. Think: "Where should I cast from? How long a line do I need? Where should my fly land? Is there going to be a drag problem?"

In fact, even with upstream casting drag can still ruin all chances of catching that feeding trout. There are two ploys which the angler still has up his sleeve. The first is to cast as slack a line as possible so that any belly will not have caused the fly to drag before it reaches the fish. The second, to employ in really difficult situations, is to cast so that the fly lands in the trout's "window".

The fish *may* take immediately: often it will not. Let me give an instance.

I was on the River Lune with Peter. We found a nice trout feeding nearer to the opposite bank and between us and it there

The Effects of Downstream and Upstream Striking

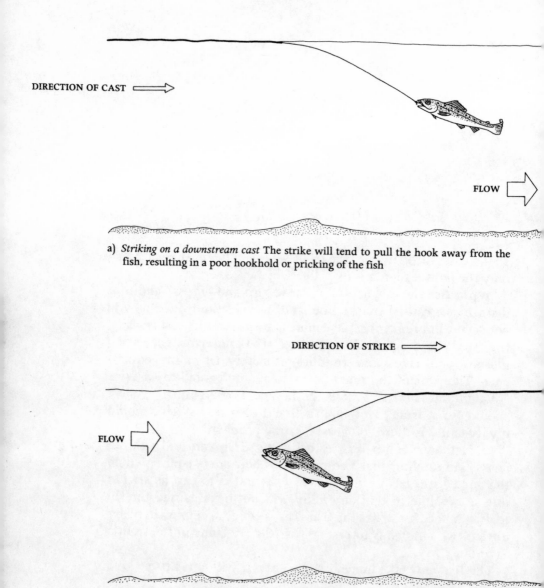

a) *Striking on a downstream cast* The strike will tend to pull the hook away from the fish, resulting in a poor hookhold or pricking of the fish

b) *Striking on an upstream cast* The strike will tend to pull the hook into the fish, resulting in a good hookhold.

were two fast flows separated by a piece of slow water. It was as complicated a cast, from the potential drag problems, as I have ever seen. Peter had a few standard upstream casts to it, but to no avail. Immediate drag! But the fish was not disturbed and kept on taking olive duns from the surface. Then I cast a very slack line to it, hoping that the fly would reach the fish before drag pulled the fly across the river. No good! Still drag ruined the cast. "What a drag!" we joked as we sat and watched. Then a daddy-long-legs plopped onto the river right over the trout and, in a swirl, it vanished. Quickly, I removed the Greenwell, tied on a dry Daddy-long-legs and plopped it also directly over the trout. It took immediately!

3. Earlier I mentioned some experiments I carried out, using wet flies, in frequency of offers and percentage of success. Rarely, when casting downstream, are more than 70% of offers success-ful in that a fish is landed. Many trout are "pricked"; hookholds are poor. Frequently the fly falls out of the trout's mouth after it has been landed. So poor is the hooking power of the down-stream cast. Offers to upstream casts are more easily connected with, provided the offers are detected when subsurface flies are used (see later) and the hookhold is much better. In 1984 and 1985 I landed 427 trout from 451 offers on upstream casts (about 95%).

The reason for the high success of upstream casts is obvious. When the angler "strikes" to a downstream offer there is a tendency to pull the fly away from the trout's mouth. In an upstream cast the hook is pulled, on the strike, into the trout's mouth.

4. It has been said before and I will say it again here, for I believe it to be true; generally a downstream cast, resulting in a dragging fly attracts mainly the smaller trout which are less discerning than the older, larger fish.

I suspect that the downstream cast would have been largely abandoned if it had not been necessary to supplement the wild trout stocks with fish reared in trout farms. Such "stockies" know nothing of real trout food and it takes them some time to become accustomed to what is food and what is not food in the river. They are readily attracted by rapid movements of small trout flies when fished with an unnatural drag and they are easily taken by this method. So stupid are these stockies that, should one be hooked on one team of three flies, then the rest of the shoal in that pool will follow the hooked fish whilst it is being played out and frequently grab at the two other flies on the cast. Thus it is not unusual for two or three of these fish to come to the net at once.

For me this is not trout angling. It is more akin to "feathering" for mackerel in the sea! However, for a lot of anglers this is considered good sport. Hence they use the dragging wet fly in early spring to "catch their fair share of the stocked trout" and never change when the remnants of the stockies become wilder, or only the native trout are left. If that is your style, well and good! But it is not of this sort of artificial sport that this book deals.

Finally whilst on the subject of up versus downstream casting, let me scotch, once and for all, the proud boast so often made by those using teams of wet flies cast across and down the stream: that they are fishing the traditional northern wet fly style. This is absolute rubbish.

T. E. Pritt was the master of the northern wet fly school and in 1885 in *Yorkshire Wet Flies* and in 1886 in *North Country Flies* he described how the northern wet fly should be fished. He put it this way:

"to fish downstream in a clear water is to court both disappointment and ridicule."

Why disappointment? Surely because fewer fish will be caught than when fishing upstream.

Why ridicule? Surely because it was accepted practice amongst northern wet fly specialists of the late 19th century to cast upstream; and that if someone fished downstream he was considered a laughing stock!

Later two other great Yorkshire anglers described the ground rules for fishing the northern "downstream" wet fly "style"; Harfield Edmonds and Norman Lee in *Brook and River Trouting* (1916). They put it this way:

"There are two methods of fishing the wet fly, upstream and downstream.

PLATE 7

LARGE DRY FLIES

Black Palmered Sedge

Deerhair Sedge

Brown Palmered Sedge (winged)

Aire Mayfly Dun

Aire Mayfly Spinner

Daddy-long-legs

Brown Moth

AUTUMN SPECIALS

Sturdy's Fancy

Treacle Parkin

Red Tag

PLATE 8

He's on. Well-hooked but not yet ready for the net.

The use of the word 'downstream' in this connection is, perhaps, somewhat misleading, for it is not intended to refer to that method of fishing in which the angler casts his flies across and downstream, allowing the current to sweep them round to a point below him, in the same manner as when fishing the salmon fly. To fish an imitation of a natural insect in such a way as to make it resist the onward flow of the water in a most unnatural manner, is, in the writers' judgement, unsound, and they wish it to be understood that, by 'downstream', they do not allude to this manner of fishing.

The downstream method advocated might quite appropriately be termed across-stream fishing, as the angler faces the bank towards which he proposes fishing, casts *across and slightly upstream* (my italics), then allows the flies to be carried without drag till they reach a point a few yards below where they alighted on the water. The only reason for the term "downstream" being used in connection with this class of fishing is that the angler himself works downstream.

The next question for consideration is, when is downstream fishing advisable? It may truly be answered, 'Not often.'"

"Not often" suggests exceptions, and the exceptions are these. When obstructions, such as riverside vegetation, prevents an up-and-across cast. When the trout's lie is surrounded by protruding boulders on the downstream side and the only way to get a fly to the fish is by floating it down into the lie. When a downstream gale prevents a cast up into the lie.

There is one other exception that I shall deal with more fully in Chapter 8. And that is when the river is clearing after a spate and the trout are lying in the slacker water out of the main flow and preying on lesser fish. Then a sea trout or lake fly, such as a small Peter Ross or Silver March Brown, can be used to good effect cast downstream and worked slowly back through the slack water. However, one should check carefully the fishing rules to ensure that such a method is allowed.

Dry Fly Fishing
Dry Fly is basically the easiest form of fly fishing for trout as every aspect of the technique is visibly obvious. A trout is seen

to breach the water surface and the angler moves stealthily upstream towards it. The next step is to watch the river surface and identify what flies are floating downstream. None may be obvious, but a close examination may reveal dead spent spinners or land flies lying flat on the surface film. If there are definitely none then one must presume that the fish had taken either a nymph from just below the water surface or an odd fly that happened to float past.

To hurry things and bombard the fish with a randomly-chosen artificial fly in this early stage is to court disaster and put the fish down. If at all possible the potential prey must be identified as closely as possible and this identification confirmed by watching the fish take another fly whilst under close observation.

Then it is a simple matter to choose an appropriate imitation from the fly box. The fly is then cast so that it lands as lightly as possible on the flow just a couple of feet or so (depending upon the likelyhood of drag) above the trout. Slack line is gathered in as the fly drifts down over the lie. If there is no response then the fly is lifted from the river, dried with a couple of false casts aimed well downstream behind the fish and recast. More often than not, if the artificial is ignored more than three times then the artificial is not good enough or something else is wrong. So, watch the fish until it takes another natural fly: then you will be sure that you have not disturbed it. Tie on an alternative pattern and try that.

If you have tried a couple of imitations of the fly on which the fish is feeding to no success then something else is wrong. The first is that there is some slight, almost imperceptible drag which destroys the illusion that the fur-and-feather concoction tied to the hook *is* a real fly. Move a few yards up or downstream to change the angle of attack, cast the fly closer to the fish or even right over the fish. That may help (see earlier in this chapter).

The second possible cause of failure in this situation is what I call the Floating Leader Syndrome! The nylon leader point is floating causing a line of disturbance to the fly and possibly glistening in the sun. On hard-fished waters there is no doubt that this is a major cause of trout rejecting the dry fly. Often they can be seen to rise to the fly and turn away at the last moment: the sure sign of F. L. S.!

What did you do wrong then? In your haste you forgot to degrease the leader point.

Make it a rule always to rub some sinkant on the leader point before making your first cast to a new fish and after handling the leader point. It may seem a bit niggley to have to rummage in your pocket for a bottle of sinkant, to anoint the line and then put away the bottle before making a cast to that trout which is awaiting *your* fly. But making this a routine is well worth it. I am sure, that over the years, it has increased the size of my catch significantly.

So, at last, everything comes right. The fly floats without drag, the nylon point does not offend and the fish takes the fly. You wait until the fish turns down towards its lie and lift the rod: the fish is hooked. If you cannot see what is going on beneath the surface you give it a second, maybe two, to turn down and you tighten: the fish is hooked! But no matter what, you must allow the trout time to turn down before you tighten. Some anglers shout "God Save the Queen!" when the fish takes the fly and tighten on the word "Queen". I have found that I say "And tighTEN", and I tighten on the "TEN". Be too quick and you will pull the fly out of the trout's open mouth; be too slow and the fish will have spat it out. Always err on the slow side. Being too quick is fatal.

Incidentally two "bewares"!

Beware of "fishing the water" with dry fly for long periods or casting time and time again to a reluctant fish. Mechanical casting like this removes the brain's concentration on the job in hand. So, should an offer come, the reaction is often an irrational reflex and too quick. An offer is thus missed. Each cast should be carefully considered so that the brain will respond in a controlled manner. Splash . . . "And tighTEN" . . . fish on.

Beware of "striking". We should not strike: i.e. move the rod up quickly. Cod fishermen on Spurn Point "strike". They need to. They have to set a big hook in the jaw of a big fish. They can do. They are using very strong line. But when river trouting we are using hooks around size 14 and nylon of very low breaking strain. All the trout angler need do is tighten sufficiently so that the tiny hook takes a hold in the trout's jaw. A slow lift of the rod. A turn of the wrist. Oliver Kite put it this way, "Feel for the fish".

Wet fly and unweighted nymph

It is not unusual to fish two or three wet flies on one cast so that the fish are given a "choice" of fly. This is especially the case when fishing the river and not casting to a particular identified trout. In this latter case it is generally better to fish a single fly or nymph. The use of more than one fly can present problems of tangle and the extra hooks attaching onto underwater snags, so that it is better to stick to the one fly whenever possible.

When casting wet fly or nymph to a particular fish the technique is exactly the same as when dry fly fishing except that the fly is not always taken with a swirl or splashing rise at the water surface. Intense concentration is therefore needed to detect the offer. This is easy enough when the water is very clear and the fish can be seen actually taking the wet fly or nymph. Then the setting of the hook can be carefully timed to coincide with the trout having the fly in its mouth. You can actually see the fish turn towards your fly. As it opens its mouth to suck in the fly the white inside of the mouth will appear and then the white gape will disappear as the trout closes its mouth on the fly. *Then* is the time to strike. Wait a second longer and there will be a flash of white as the trout opens its mouth and rejects the fly. But except for the clear chalkstreams and limestone becks this may often be impossible: the fish may be barely visible or not visible at all. Sometimes there might be the flash of a trout beneath the surface as it takes a fly and an immediate tightening often results in success. But more usually the only indication of an offer is from the leader and tip of the fly line.

To enhance indications of subsurface offers it is beneficial to carry out some treatment of the terminal part of the line. Firstly the leader and droppers should be degreased with sinkant. Then with Permagrease the end of the fly line and leader butt are heavily greased. Finally, before casting, the nymph or wet flies are wetted with saliva so that they penetrate the water easily. When a trout takes there are several possible indications: the line might halt momentarily in its downstream drift; the greased leader butt and fly line might twitch, dart upstream for an inch or more, or dip quickly beneath the surface. To any of these the angler must respond *immediately* by raising the rod quickly. For when the indication is noticed the fly is already in the trout's mouth and a split-second later it will have been rejected. So intense concentration and fast reactions are essential. Certainly the fish rarely hook themselves with upstream wet fly or nymph, a factor which encourages the irrational and fairly widespread use of the downstream wet fly. But as I explained earlier in this chapter, the advantages of fishing upstream greatly outweigh this one apparent disadvantage.

Weighted Nymph

Two anglers published books describing nymph fishing, both from the chalkstream: Frank Sawyer in *Nymphs and the Trout* and Oliver Kite in *Nymph Fishing in Practice*. I would strongly recommend all trout anglers to buy, beg or borrow copies of these classic works. These weighted nymphs can be used to catch trout no matter at what depth they have been observed feeding but are, from my experience, most suited to taking trout that are feeding deep. I invariably use such nymphs when the trout are not breaking or moving close to the water surface.

The basic idea is that the nymph is pitched or cast into the river upstream of a trout that is grubbing in weed beds or river-bed gravel. The nymph sinks very quickly and passes the trout at its feeding depth. Offers are indicated in exactly the same way as they are in standard wet fly and nymph fishing; the angler must respond quickly if he is to hook his fish.

There is one additional ruse when using the weighted nymph that can cause or induce a reluctant trout to take it: the "induced take". As the nymph drifts downstream in front or alongside the trout the angler raises the rod tip. This movement causes the nymph to rise through the water in a very life-like manner. Invariably the trout will respond. So effective is the induced take that many anglers, confident of the location of a feeding trout that they cannot actually see, have learnt that if they tighten immediately after causing the nymph to lift in front of the trout, as if by magic the trout is hooked. But so consistently effective

97

is the induced take that the late Oliver Kite apparently used to catch trout for observers with it, with a bag over his head so that there was no way he could see offers. What an incredible party trick!

Such events suggest that with the weighted nymph, many offers are not easily seen. The reactions of the greased leader butt to an offer, which can be quite marked in subsurface wet fly or nymph angling (see above) are much less strong. Mere flicks or the slightest twitches: almost none. Of course if one can see the fish in the water there is no difficulty, for one sees it take the nymph.

Only two weighted nymphs are required, something which removes much of the "which fly should I use" and "should I change my fly" syndromes from which dry fly and wet fly anglers are often prone to suffer. The best is Sawyer's Pheasant Tail Nymph (Kite used only this one) in sizes 16 and 14. The other which I use, also devised by Sawyer, is the Killer Bug which, in sizes 14 and 12, adequately represents shrimps and the water hog-louse.

Coarse fish are an excellent source of practice, during the trout close season, for the newcomer to the weighted nymph. Take some to a water holding a lot of roach, chub or dace and give them a try. Alternatively find a shoal of grayling in winter, by using worming tackle, and then try the Killer Bug with the induced take method. Persevere; gain some confidence in the technique. And you too will be able to amaze your angling friends by demonstrating this little used but effective method. And have a go at emulating Oliver Kite: do the demonstration blindfolded.

CHAPTER SIX

Early Spring : March and April

"The angler's year may be divided into three stages. The first . . . is marked by rises which begin and end suddenly . . ."

John Waller Hills. *A Summer on the Test.* 1930.

In most areas of Britain the trout-fishing season commences in March though in others the first of April is the great day, whilst on a few waters opening day is put back to the middle of that month or even to the first of May. Possibly the fifteenth of March, when the season opens on my own rivers of northern England, is a little too early. The brown trout, which have spawned in the coldest days of November and December, are often still recovering from the rigours of breeding. Many are still very lean and soft-bellied and lack the muscle and, consequently, fight that they would have if they were given a few extra weeks to recover completely.

The problem is that during the coldest months of the year, January and February, when water temperatures often fall close to zero degrees celsius, the metabolism of the cold-blooded inhabitants of the river is at its lowest. As a general rule a ten degree celsius increase in temperature results in a doubling of the physiological life process of such animals. Thus energy production in the muscle and nerve cells of trout, by which the fish seeks out the food necessary to replenish its tissues that have wasted away during the mating season, is at its lowest in the weeks following that weakening annual event. By the end of April, when water temperatures should, in a good year, have risen by at least ten degrees the trout has at least twice the energy available for searching for food than it had in the cold water of late winter. Furthermore the same also applies to the small fish (usually minnows and miller's thumbs) and invertebrates on which the trout feeds in the river pools. They too are less active in the low water temperatures of late winter and early spring; many invertebrates even appear to hibernate through low temperature conditions. Thus what food is present in the river will be less conspicuous by its lack of activity to the lethargic trout. So debilitating are low water temperatures that many invertebrates over-winter as minute eggs, fertilised and laid in the water the previous late summer or autumn. Once the water temperature has risen to a reasonable level then these eggs will hatch, the inhabitants of the river will resume feeding and growing, and for the trout there will be an increasing food supply upon which it can feed. Thus while trout can be in quite poor condition in late February or early March, come early April and the same fish are in prime condition.

Incidentally this temperature effect on cold-blooded organisms is of course widespread. Thus there are many instances of the inability of running salmon to make progress through a length of rough white-water or over waterfalls until the water has reached a certain temperature. At lower temperatures their nerve-muscles do not generate sufficient energy to accomplish the task. Likewise when salmon-fishing in spring the best "taking-time" is around mid-day or early afternoon when the slight increase of water temperature results, through increased energy levels, in an increasing alertness in the salmon's sensory system. This is somewhat similar to a case I met frequently as a small boy on the dunes of south Lancashire in the 1950s. At the time, before the "development" of this fine length of coastline between Southport and Liverpool during the 1960s and early 1970s, these dunes had large colonies of both common and sand lizards. Alas the latter are very rare there now. On hot summer days we found it very difficult to catch the lizards. The slightest quick movement on our part and they were off; both sensory system and muscle system were in tip-top form as they basked in the hot sun. But if we could find sand lizards out and about on a cool, cloudy day then catching them was easy; they were much more lethargic.

So, the river temperatures in early spring will affect the activities of invertebrates and the trout, and also the condition of the trout. Following a mild late winter the fish and invertebrates may be very active; the trout in excellent condition. But following a typical prolonged cold spell in late winter, dominated by frost and snow, the trout may be in quite a poor condition and not really worthy quarry before April.

Of course many fisheries overcome the problem of uncertain quality of the over-wintered fish during the first weeks of the season by stocking the river with fish raised in stew-ponds where, through the provision of high protein pellets, the stock trout that have not spawned are kept feeding. There is, alas, a problem of such early season stocking especially when the fish are tipped, in large numbers, into water of very low temperatures. As I have already explained, there is little natural food available for the trout. Yet the stockies are used to food being supplied, in large amounts, once or twice a day. They are put into the river pools in small shoals and, come feeding time, they expectantly await the food to be thrown in. But it does not come. So they move, usually downstream, in search of food; which, of course, they do not find. And they keep on going. Thus this early stocking may be entirely lost to those that put the fish in the river, for rapidly they wander down to other beats where others receive the benefit.

I remember well my own club carrying out an experimental early-season stocking of a beat on the upper Lune. Three days later five of us visited the water and found that not one stockie remained. Similarly a beat on the River Hodder was heavily stocked, one year, in conditions of low cold water. Within two days the whole stocking of several hundred trout was several miles downstream. On another similar occasion, on the River Wenning (a tributary of the Lune) two of us watched as our stock fish drifted down with the flow from pool to pool until, eventually, they left our beat. The early stocking of rivers is somewhat of a gamble especially on those smaller spate rivers of northern England where the rapid variation of water level renders the water temperature to react rapidly to the air temperature. It seems less of a problem on the spring-fed chalk streams where

101

flow-rate and water temperature are kept fairly constant by the reservoir of water held in the huge underground chalk reservoirs. Losses of stock fish are also less in northern spate rivers where the beat that is stocked has pools that are large, very deep and with a sluggish flow; possibly because such pools resemble more the character of the stew-ponds whence the fish originated.

Because of the effects of temperature early spring trouting can be disappointing. This is characterised by lethargic trout, trout in poor condition and the possibility of losing stock trout that have been added to the water to provide early season angling of fish that are, unnaturally, in good fettle. Such a picture may appear somewhat pessimistic; but unless the winter has been mild and rainfall sufficient to maintain a good flow of relatively warm water it is correct. Hence my suggestion that on many rivers an opening day before April is too early. However we must remember that the close season for brown trout is the longest close season for any fish species: as near as makes any difference, six months or half year. For the keen fisherman for brown trout it has been a very long wait! So, he may have spent some of the time fishing stillwaters for rainbow trout. But such is third-rate sport compared with river trouting. He may have made regular visits to the river for grayling, an anomalous species that comes into its prime in the cold short days of winter. He may have fished for salmon through to the previous November and from late January and February. Yet fishing for these, fine quarry that they are, does not compare for many anglers with the art of river trouting. Thus on the opening day we find the keenest trout anglers on their favourite beats no matter what the weather and despite the possibility of the fishing being not particularly good.

There is no doubt that the majority of food taken by trout throughout the entire season is obtained from below the water surface. Even those fish that are observed to take a floating dun or spent spinner from the surface and which are taken on a dry fly often have guts which contain, predominantly, items of food that have been taken either just below the water surface (usually hatching nymphs or pupae) or from the depths close to the river bed. In northern waters the latter are often dominated by caddis larvae grubbed from the riverbed or from amongst aquatic mosses which clothe the more static boulders. In weedy chalk streams or the more alkaline spate rivers where there are weed beds, usually in the form of water crowfoot (or water buttercup), water hog louse, water shrimps, snails and swimming ephemerid nymphs comprise the bulk of the food. But the easiest and usual way of catching river trout in early spring is by seeking out those fish that are feeding either just below or at the water surface: fish that are easy to locate as they swirl to take a nymph as it reaches the surface film or break the surface to remove the floating fly. Later in the year, when the brighter light and cleaner, lower water permit better visibility into the depths one can angle for the deep-feeding trout by using weighted flies. But why bother in spring, when the trout are so obliging at or close to the surface?

In chalkstreams this has meant dry fly since the revolution in angling brought about by F. M. Halford and G. S. Marryat. Even the previous and subsequent developers of the chalkstream nymph method (G. E. M. Skues, O. Kite and F. Sawyer) acknowledged that in spring dry fly reigns supreme. In the spate rivers in the north and west of Britain the fishing of early spring involves two contrasting styles: dry fly and sub-surface wet fly. Alas the latter which has dominated the "northern style" for generations is a much ill-used way of angling: a chuck-and-chance" it way of fishing—a style of fishing that appears to differ from salmon and sea trout fishing only by the small size of the flies that are used. But when fished with care and thought, upstream, to bulging trout that are obviously taking nymphs and pupae just below the water surface, it is an exciting and efficient method of angling. When fished in the traditional "down-and-across" and "step-and-cast" style it is an abysmally tedious way of catching trout.

I say tedious because in early spring, certainly from April, there are often good hatches of two or three species of fly on which the trout are keen to feed. How irrational is the fisherman who flogs his way down a pool with his flies skating unnaturally at high speed across the flow whilst around him trout are leisurely taking duns and emerging nymphs at the water surface.

It might be thought that I am exaggerating: believe me I am

not! Consider the following instance. Two friends were fishing a superb northern spate river beat one beautiful late April day. The trout were taking olive duns. Eight other anglers were fishing the two pools and intervening run. They were spaced well out along the bank, wading as deep as they could (Why? Some of the trout were rising closer to the bank than these anglers) and whipping their wet flies back as quickly as they could. Then a pace and another cast . . . and so on. As the queue proceeded, the one lowest down the river would, upon reaching the end of the pool, emerge and walk up the back to join the tail of the queue. The two friends cast dry fly to selected fish whenever a gap appeared in the queue. The result: they had eight trout in a couple of hours; not one of the queue of eight downstream wet fly anglers landed a fish.

Too many anglers of the northern wet fly school spend too much time actually fishing (or rather casting). They do not spend enough time on the riverbank simply watching the river. Yet a fish seen feeding should, in most situations, be easily caught in spring. An olive dun floats downstream, a trout breaks the flat unruffled water. A suitably sized Imperial or Greenwell's Glory is tied to the leader point. The fish takes another olive. A careful cast, an offer, the strike . . . the fish is yours provided the strike is timed well and the hookhold is a reasonable one. The same applies to the use of upstream wet fly or nymph; the way sunk fly should be used. It is that easy. I have no doubt that if most anglers spent less time on their feet by the river, waded into the water only when this was essential (i.e. rarely) and spent the majority of the day watching and thinking they would more than double their catch rate.

This was brought home to me forceably several years ago when I was fortunate enough to spend some days in the company of one of England's finest tyers of flies and trout anglers, Jack Norris. Few readers will have heard of Jack, certainly outside the rivers of Lancashire. He is one of the most unassuming and generous of anglers that one might meet. Yet to spend a day with him in spring is an education. Let me give one typical example.

It is a beautiful early spring day as Jack arrives at the bridge at 9 o'clock and walks over the hill to save scrambling on the steep riverside path through the wood. Several anglers are already on the river, wading up to their knees and throwing their teams of wet flies as far as they can down and across the flow. Jack waves to them as he passes. Eventually he reaches his chosen perch, on a grassy sward which commands a good view of two decent pools. We meet him there and sit down for a chat. We tackle up, have a drink from the Thermos flask and talk of the water conditions and prospects for the day. "Twelve thirty or one o'clock today" says Jack as he sits back in the sun and lights a cigarette.

Occasionally a couple of anglers of the random wet fly pass, as they step-and-cast their way along the apparently fishless river. They stop and say hello and, in response to our enquiry, tell us of "three good pulls and lost a good 'un". But despite the number of anglers working hard, only the occasional trout has been netted. At 12.45 a splashing rise from a trout upstream of us signifies the start of the hatch. We examine the flow; the first hatch of the day's spring olives is trundling along the flow. There is a swirl and one of them vanishes. Jack now springs into action; his long carbon fly rod flexes as the delicate olive imitation is pitched just upstream of the trout's position. There is another swirl, Jack raises his rod, the trout is hooked and soon is in the net. As more olives float downstream, more trout come onto feed and, within the hour, Jack has cast to six others, hooked them all and landed five. The hatch peters out over the next hour; a few fish show at the surface even when the hatch has stopped. But by five o'clock it is all over for the day. Jack leaves the river and, for the minimum of exertion, has had more trout than all of the anglers combined on his beat.

It is an unnerving experience, but it always works. Geoff Haslam and I arrived on the riverside one April morning: the river had been stocked a week or so before. Two other anglers were already fishing the pool. "Waste of time!" we were told. "We have been here since dawn and haven't touched a fish. The stockies must have been hammered. It's a dead loss and we're going home!"

And home they went. Geoff and I sat by the river watching the water surface. Nothing stirred from the depths. Then through the shallow river into the top pool we spotted a fluttering as a spring olive beat its wings as it rushed along the flow. As it reached the neck of the pool there was a splash and, hey-presto, the fly had vanished. Over the next hour a steady stream of flies followed the path of the pioneer and the trout, that had been lying motionless and ignoring the dragging wet flies of the two departed anglers responded. Our sport was fast, furious and exciting until eventually, the hatch dried up and the fish went down once more. I have given these examples which are characteristic of the best in early spring trout fishing, to demonstrate that if the trout are not feeding, it can be a pretty futile exercise in trying to catch them. So, the odd trout can be caught in the early spring at the crack of dawn or at dusk. But the angler's energies should be concentrated on the magic hours from about lunch time to teatime when there is a hatch of fly and the trout are induced to feed.

Throughout the river systems of Britain, two flies are most important to the trout and trout angler in early spring. One I have already referred to: the large dark spring olive, the most ubiquitous of the ephemerids. The second is less abundant and less widespread, but still of great importance, the iron blue. There is a third ephemerid that is extremely local in its distribution but, where it occurs it is of great importance: the true march brown. Small midges might be on the water on particularly warm days and the fish may feed keenly on these. But they are too tiny to imitate realistically. And in any case the trout will invariably turn their attention to the ephemerids once they begin to hatch. Likewise a couple of stonefly species hatch from the cleanest of northern and western hill streams but these can be largely ignored for, as was explained in Chapter 3, the stoneflies never hatch at the water surface but crawl ashore through the riverbed boulders unseen by the trout.

Flies of Early Spring
The identification of these three important species of flies is fairly straightforward provided the angler sits down, minus rod, and watches for a few minutes:

Large Dark (Spring) Olive Dun: a medium-sized fly with wings about 1·5 centimeters in length, a fairly uniform blue-grey and held upright; hatch occurs persistently between noon and about 4.00 p.m. with a peak emergence 12.30–2.30 p.m. The most widespread and common early spring fly.

Iron Blue Dun: a smallish fly (wings about 1 cm in length) with overall an inky blue-black colouration; the wings appear to be held at a more rakish angle compared with the large olive; hatch occurs in the afternoon between noon and 4.00 p.m.

True March Brown Dun: a large fly (wings up to 2 cm. long, which are mottled cream and brown and held at a rakish angle compared with the large olive). The hatch generally occurs between 11.00 a.m. and 3.00 p.m. and is quite characteristic, coming in waves with lulls in between. This species occurs only on the rough, rocky, fast rivers of the north and west such as the Usk, Eden, Nith and Deveron but is, curiously, absent from other apparently suitable waters. Also on one particular river its distribution can be patchy and thus, whilst it may be abundant along one length, a couple of miles away it may be rare or absent.

No matter what the river or stream, if it holds brown trout it will also have the large olive and that is thus the one fly for the novice to angling-entomology to expect and look for. Then if, at about the same time another smaller dark fly appears it will be the iron blue. Finally, if fishing a rough, rocky, northern, west-country or Welsh river the third member of the trio might appear. This illustrates the point I made in Chapter 3, that there is often no great need for complicated keys, dissecting instrument, hand nets and a microscope.

In these flies of early spring the dun is *the* important stage for the angler, save possibly for the true march brown spinner (also called the great red spinner) that can, sometimes, fall on the water in large numbers after mating and egg laying. So, basically, we need in this period dry flies and wet flies to imitate the three duns and the one spinner.

Flies to imitate the Large Olive dun
    Dry (size 14):   Kite's Imperial, Greenwell's Glory (modified), M. G. Olive.
    Wet (size 12 or 14): Waterhen Bloa (I will offer no other for there is no need to. This is the best wet imitation of the large olive).

Flies to imitate the Iron Blue dun
    Dry (size 16):   M. G. Iron Blue.
    Wet (size 14 or 16): Snipe and Purple, Dark Watchet

Flies to imitate the March Brown dun
    Dry (size 12):   Woolley's Dry March Brown.
    Wet (size 12):   Woolley's Wet March Brown.
    Nymph (size 12):   Woolley's March Brown nymph.

I gave this nymph pattern because it has been recorded (though I have not witnessed this) that the nymph of the March Brown makes several trips to the surface before emerging and that the trout feed avidly on the nymphs when they are doing this. A nymph imitation might be useful if this is encountered.

Dry Fly to imitate the March Brown (great red) spinner (size 12 or 14)
    M.G. Orange Spinner

The great G. E. M. Skues wrote, of the flies representing the March Brown,

"an excellent fly, and as generally tied, quite a poor imitation of the natural fly and quite a passable one of almost anything else."

Thus on many occasions the trout will take a March Brown even though there may be none in or on the water. They may take it as a general nymph or olive imitation; they may take it

PLATE 9

Waiting for the evening rise in high summer and the river low.

There is the temptation to start fishing before the fish start feeding. This is usually a mistake. A premature start may disturb some fish that might be catchable later. And time spent in a careful reconnaissance will allow you to choose an artificial fly that matches the natural flies on the water and enables you to spot feeding trout and think about the best way of getting your fly to them.

A brace of brown trout (2 lb. 3 oz. and 2 lb. 1 oz.) taken between midnight and 1.30 am. on a dry sedge.

PLATE 10

Can I recommend the use of barbless hooks? Here the author releases a trout by simply sliding the point and bend of the hook from its jaw.

To remove a barbed hook the trout may have to be handled with traumatic and possible fatal consequences.

Peter Greenhalgh taking full advantage of what little cover there is.

as an imitation of the water shrimp or water hog louse. Or whatever. It is a general, useful fly.

The same applies to one other fly that I find indispensable during early spring, the Orange Partridge. This has always been a favourite on northern rivers but what the fish take it for is hard to understand. At one time it was said to represent the small stonefly, the February red (a local species which is not, in any case, out and about in April). They may take it for a nymph or shrimp or, as with the various March Brown patterns, a general item of food. But certainly, if I am fishing a team of wet flies in spring this pattern is invariably on my cast.

In fact to suggest an early spring wet fly trout cast one could do little better than the following: Orange Partridge, Waterhen Bloa, and Snipe and Purple or Dark Watchet. I also remember successful days I had with these flies. Here's one short account of two of them.

The first one was on a warm, bright, sunny spring day on the upper Ribble. The 15th of March. And, although I had been fishing for grayling throughout the long months and short days of winter I was eager to be off, for the start of the brown trout season signifies, as much as anything, the beginning of the best six months of the year. The day was so pleasant, promising the warmth of spring and the heat of summer to come. So, I was by the river fairly early (at 9 o'clock). I took two rods. I set one with dry fly, size 14 Kite's Imperial, for the post-lunch hatch of olives. On the other I put my standard cast of three wet flies: Orange Partridge, Waterhen Bloa and Dark Watchet. Then I walked slowly upstream.

The neck of the Bridge Pool was inviting so, leaving bag and rod by an old sycamore stump, I made my way onto the shingle. Slowly I lengthened line and the flies fell upstream of me into the fast flow. As the cast was fished out I stripped off more line and cast further up and across. As the flies drifted down there was a momentary stop and twitch of the tip of the floating line. I lifted and was into my first trout of the year: a good fish that swam down into the pool, taking some slack line as it did so. A few moments later I netted out a nice fish of about a pound and in quite good condition considering the date. It had seized upon the Waterhen Bloa. I killed this and proceeded further up the river. By the time I reached the tail of the next pool I had another four fish; three leaner specimens which I shook from the hook to fatten up and another good one of at least a pound. Three took the Waterhen Bloa and the fourth the Orange Partridge.

I moved upstream disturbing a pre-breeding party of eight oystercatchers that were dozing on the riverside pastures, and came to the weir. Here I sat and had a cup of coffee whilst I watched a pair of dippers flitting up and down the river with nest material. Behind me curlew, lapwing, snipe and redshank were displaying on the wet pastures. It was 11.30 p.m.; not a fish moved. So I had an early lunch and watched the birds. At 12.20 p.m. a trout splashed in the weir pool but I could see no flies drifting downwater. Thinking that it might have taken an early dun or nymph close to the surface, I decided to give it a few throws with the wet flies. It took on the third cast and hooked itself: a fine fish that bored quickly across the fast flow below the little weir before it became airborne as it proceeded downwater. Soon I had it in the deep water at my feet and had it netted out. The best fish so far. Well over the pound mark. It was 12.50 p.m. before the olive duns appeared, drifting down-water with wings held high and the hatch, a good one, lasted until about 2.30 p.m. Through this period I turned to the dry fly rod and I suppose I cast to nine or ten fish. One was a grayling of around the two pound mark (I invariably catch a good grayling on the first day of the close season!). Five trout also came to the net of which I retained one and returned the other four; I missed the offer from two fish. All were on the Imperial. At 3.00 p.m. I slowly made my way downwater but, as I did so, saw five fish move at or close to the water surface. To these I cast the wet flies. Two offers I missed, one fish ignored my flies, the two others I hooked, landed and returned for they were in need of a few weeks feeding before they would be in top condition. Both took the Waterhen Bloa. It had been a fine day.

The second day was one in mid-April on the Lune. During the morning, from about 8.30 a.m. I fished wet flies upstream into likely lies: the necks of pools, deeper runs below trees and the edges of back eddies. In three hours I had landed five brownies, of which I retained two, and missed three offers. Three fish took the Orange Partridge, one the Dark Watchett and one the Waterhen Bloa. Then, between 12.15 and 3.30 p.m. there was a good hatch of spring olives with just a sprinkling of iron blue duns. Five fish took the dry imitation of the olive (three to the MG Olive and two to the Imperial). Two, that were seen to take the iron blues refused the olive but took the MG Iron Blue: one I lost and the second, the best fish of the day, I kept. With the hatch over I returned to the wet fly and had two fish from the neck of our best pool, both on the Dark Watchet. Another superb day with the best fish scaling 2 lb. 6 oz. But on this day the iron blue imitations were more significant due to the presence of that little fly on the river.

There have been days where the fish have refused the olive imitations, both wet and dry, and been feeding selectively on iron blues. One day, on the River Wharfe, and fishing my standard spring wet fly cast, all the trout that I caught came to the Snipe & Purple: the Orange Partridge and Waterhen Bloa were ignored. On another occasion, this time on the River Annan, I encountered a massive sporadic hatch of true march browns and, once more, the fish were selective, five taking the wet March Brown and two the Orange Partridge.

Whenever one fishes for brown trout in these early weeks of the season then at least one of these ephemerids will almost certainly dominate the days fishing. On a few occasions I have had days where, for some reason, the trout have ignored the large wholesome food items and insisted on feeding exclusively on the tiniest of pale grey midges. When this has happened they have driven me close to despair. I have even tied imitations of these midges on size 26 hooks but they have been ignored; they were too large. I am sorry, but when they are up to this there is nothing we can do but suffer.

111

CHAPTER SEVEN

Late Spring : May to Mid-June

"The river at any season is interesting, but towards the end of May, when the hawthorn is laden with its covering of fragrant snow and the beech hedges in the country lanes are tender green, we find its attractions beyond description. The trout, too, revel in this season. . . ."

R. C. Bridgett. *By Loch and Stream*. 1922.

Beyond any doubt the second half of spring is the best period within the half-year brown trout fishing season. Not only are the variety and quantity of fly hatches better than at any other part of the season, but the brown trout are in their prime. Fish that remain from early spring stockings have lost much of their naivety and become wary of the angler and his tackle; many will have fallen for the anglers lure before and been returned to the river, unharmed physically but conscious of the fact that they are a hunted quarry. And these remaining stockies will have become accustomed to real trout river foods. They will be selecting the various invertebrates and diminutive fish that are the fare of the wild trout. They will also have acquired lies, small areas of river which provide cover and, simultaneously, guide a steady stream of food, borne by the fast flow through the trout's area of view or "window". A narrow gulch between two large boulders, beneath swaying thick fronds of water buttercup, beneath the overhanging lower branches of a riverside sycamore that trail in the water, beneath an undercut clay riverbank: such are typical lies.

With the huge amounts of trout foods being produced by the

river in late spring the wild fish, that at the start of the season may not have fully recovered from the rigours of spawning, rapidly regain their fitness and grow quickly. Indeed, so good is the feeding in this period that I have known stock brownies (identified by characteristic ragged or malformed fins), that have been put in the river at around the pound and a half mark in April, reaching two pounds by the middle of June.

Trout are gluttons in this period of plenty. Provided that the night is not too cold they will feed the clock round. If there is a fall of spinners in the early hours they will be devoured. Then if there are hatches of ephemerid duns through the day the trout will feed on them. And if there is a hatch of sedges in the evening they will be taken. In between time a hatch of midges will often provide a snack between meals; or the trout will grub about in the weed or boulders of the riverbed for caddis larvae, stonefly and ephemerid nymphs, snails and crustaceans. Finally, should a senseless minnow or miller's thumb stray into the trout's lie it will be added to the generous natural buffet.

Sometimes the river trout will appear to be fairly selective: but this generally happens when there is a massive hatch of one species, such as the hawthorn fly and mayfly (see later). And often, when they *appear* to be fastidious as to their selected food species the successful angler is frequently taken by surprise when he examines the gut contents of the fish in his creel. I recall one day, for example, when I extracted from the River Aire, after much effort, a brace of trout that had seemingly been exclusively taking medium olives despite several other species of fly being also on the water. The guts of these trouts were crammed with caddis, a wide variety of nymphs, black terrestrial beetles that had, presumably, been blown onto the water, and, in one, a couple of fresh water shrimps, besides the few olive duns that I had seen them taking.

However, no matter how selective the trout are in their feeding, it is a rare day, in late spring, when the competent angler scores a "blank". The flies that are out-and-about are not too difficult to imitate. And so with an initial careful spell of observation, the correct choice of fly, a stealthy approach and an accurate delicate cast fish should come easily to the net.

Not only is river trouting at its best through this six-week period but also the riverside environment is at its most inviting.

The man who goes to the river just to catch fish and is oblivious to the other inhabitants of the waterside is no real angler. The true trout angler is, in reality, a naturalist whose prime interest is the fish and fish foods. It is exactly the same for the true wild-fowler: there is more to wildfowling than killing and carrying from the estuary salt marsh a huge bag of duck or geese. The vegetation, the other birds, the mudflats, the state of the tide and the weather: they are all studied by the true wildfowler. And as the wildfowler must become an integral part of the estuarine environment, so too must the angler become intimately involved with the riverside environment if he is to get the greatest satisfaction from his sport.

Let me return for a moment to wildfowling. Some years ago I was invited to a duck shoot, on the opening day, on a large estate. We arrived at one particular "drive" and, on our way to the butts from which the guns would do the shooting, had to walk through a flock of several hundred young hand-reared mallard which crowded around us, hoping for some food. Once we reached the butts the keeper and beaters turned on the poor tame ducks and forced them into flight. The slaughter of the inno-cent commenced. Comments like "A great drive", and "I got 57" passed along the line of guns. I said nothing. I could not bring myself to raise the gun.

How can such be regarded as wildfowling? The long lonely wait out in a deep salt marsh gutter, the flights of wildfowl, waders and gulls, the movements of the tide, the changing light. These are integral to a day's wildfowling. No matter if the bag remains empty. If it does not then a couple of greylag geese or two brace of widgeon are cause for celebration.

Likewise the angler in this, the most bountiful time of the year. It is not just a matter of going down to a well-stocked river and catching a lot of fish. The true angler can still be quite content with an empty creel or just one or two fish in the bag at the end of a long day. He will have noticed the dipper, grey wagtail and kingfisher as they flit along the river. He will have realised, from their behaviour, that the pair of sandpipers have their nest in a particular clump of riverside watermint, that the curlews have their young in that boggy patch of rushes. Then he will take care to disturb them as little as possible. The primroses, marsh marigolds and cowslips are noticed. He spots the footprints, in the riverside mud, of otter and deer. Such provide so much pleasure that an empty or light creel at the end of the day is nothing more than a slight embarassment. He has seen and heard so much in his day by the river that human civilisation has been relegated to the subconscious. He has enjoyed his day and not entirely because of the fishing.

As I described in the last chapter, fishing in early spring is predictable, there being hatches of one, two or three species of upwinged fly each day and the timing of the hatches can be calculated to the hour. In summer this is not so, hatches depending upon weather conditions, the height and colour of the river water and several other factors which are sometimes not related to the river at all (see Chapter 8). The late spring period is somewhat a transition between the two. Given a rainfall pattern that maintains a good height of clear water, and the sort of condition that lake fed rivers and chalkstreams are blessed with through most of the season consequent to the natural reservoirs at their sources, then angling at this time of the year can be as predictable as early spring. Almost! But with prolonged cold, wet weather as we had, for instance, in 1985, the rivers will be bank high with a lot of colour. Hatches of fly in such circumstances tend to be sparse and prolonged so that the trout fail to settle into a proper feeding pattern. Similarly, if the late spring is dominated by drought conditions and day after day of beating hot sunshine then hatches will tend to follow the summer regime, occurring between dusk and dawn; and the few daytime hatches will be short-lived because flies will be able to leave the water quickly as the low atmospheric humidity dries their wings quickly and high temperature raises their flight muscle metabolic rate. Such occurred, for example, in 1980: one of the worst late springs we have encountered in recent years as far as the trout angler is concerned.

Fortunately the two extremes are exceptional and late spring provides us with perfect conditions. Not too hot and not too cold. Not dominated by continuous drought, but not with heavy rain day after day. Blessed with light warm upstream breezes: how often, on British rivers, are the perfect winds those from the southerly sector (west, through south, to southeast). Of the last ten years in seven of them late spring was close to perfection as far as the river trout fisherman was concerned. Can't be bad!

Flies of Late Spring

Late spring sees a great proliferation of fly life on and around the river which can be most bewildering to the new-comer to river trout fishing. In many cases the angler's name for a type of fly actually often includes more than one species as far as the scientific world is concerned. As I have said before, this really does not matter. Trout are not scientists: they do not look at the length of the intercalary veins on the wings or the size of the penis lobes or whatever that a scientist looks for to separate very similar fly species. Neither needs the angler. Not initially, at any rate. Later the angler who wishes to learn more can spend some time looking for these subtle characteristics so that he can know precisely what species is hatching. Rarely will such knowledge increase his catch rate! And there is no need at all for any trout fisherman to be conned by those who have published vast lists of flies to represent every scientific species. Simplicity in fly design, flies that have the correct size, shape and general colouration are what matters. Hence the effectiveness of artificial flies such as Greenwell's Glory and Kite's Imperial!

One of the most charming stories which demonstrates the efficacy of simplicity in fly patterns is that given by the late T. C. Kingsmill Moore in his outstanding book *A Man May Fish* (1979). There was a large hatch of iron blue duns and he had had some small success on the two standard patterns, Snipe and Purple, and a dark variant of Greenwell's Glory. But he wanted to improve his catch rate ("I was, if I may use the expression, after the iron blue's blood"). So he collected some samples of the natural fly, examined them closely with a hand lens. At this point he continues the tale.

"I matched the elephant grey body exactly with a shade of heron herl, and the more olive body with mole's fur mixed with a little of the same fur dyed in picric. The legs were pretty accurately reproduced by jackdaw's throat hackle, and a furnace hen which had been given a dose of the olive dye. There remained the wings. For these I wanted a tom-tits tail, and there were

116

plenty of tom-tits in the garden, usually up to no good. It is however impossible to shoot a bird with whom one is on a social footing. My favourite cat, who thought such squeamishness nauseating, went out and in ten minutes returned with a dead tit. He did the same on another day when I was starting to tie a batch of Greenwell's, and I found I had no hen blackbird. I started to make do with coot, when there was a shadow in the window, a plop on the floor, and a hen blackbird laid at my feet. It is fair to say that he was unusually intelligent, even for a cat."

Kingsmill then describes how he tied examples of as many imitations of the iron blue as he could find in the books and then proceeded to try them.

"None was a complete failure, but none was really successful. The best were the Snipe and Purple and the small dark Greenwell, and my imitations were nearly at the bottom of the list."

Why complicate matters when there is no need to? Most fly-tyers have, on occasion, sought to improve on the standard flies that represent such-and-such a species of natural fly, or to devise flies that imitate more accurately the individual species within a group of flies that are normally represented by one general pattern. In at least 90% of such cases the new fly is no better, and often worse, than the older pattern (see, for example, my experiences of producing patterns for the false March Brown and brook dun described later in this chapter).

Let us look, then, at the list of natural flies that might occur in, on or over the river at this bountiful season, how to imitate them with our artificial flies and how to catch the trout with them.

Stoneflies
Several species may occur, the four most famous being

> Yellow Sally
> Needle Fly
> Willow Fly
> Large Stonefly

The adults of these are of minimal important to both trout and angler as the hatches are very sparse, emergence is by the nymphs crawling out of the river before the final moult and the falls of dead adults, following egg-laying, are insignificant when compared with the huge falls of sedges, upwinged flies etc. By rivers where stoneflies are abundant the angler will see lots of adults of these species: long thin flies with wings held tightly over the abdomen; almost black in colour save for the yellow sally which has a yellow or yellow-olive colour. Look at them; enjoy seeing them for they are interesting and beautiful flies. But they are of little consequence from the angling point of view.

However, in recent years, one or two professional fly-tyers and devisers of artificial flies, possibly anxious to make a name for themselves, have devised patterns to imitate these stoneflies. So, if you want to tie or buy a Yellow Sally there are patterns available. Then, if you see a yellow sally on the water and a trout takes it, use your new pattern. You may catch that fish. But a fish that takes a real yellow sally is a fish that is feeding unselectively and you will catch it just as easily on, say, a Greenwell's Glory. I know this to be true for I have fished, on over 100 days per year, over many years, rivers and streams where stoneflies are as abundant as anywhere in these islands. Not once have I failed to catch because of the trout being fastidiously hooked on adult stoneflies. (Sorry about the pun.)

The situation is different underwater where stonefly nymphs are important items in the trout diet, grubbed from the riverbed. But again, these trout are not being selective to just stonefly nymphs. Invariably they will also be feeding on the nymphs and larvae of other groups of insects; and shrimps and water-hog louse as well. So there is no need for any special stonefly imitation; any good leaded bug or nymph, such as Sawyer's Pheasant Tail Nymph or Killer Bug, will suffice.

Upwinged Flies

There may still be significant hatches in early May of the two flies of early spring: the large dark olive and the iron blue dun. But other species or types become more important:

Mayfly: the most famous of trout flies, hatching in late May and early June (26 May–20 June are extreme dates on the rivers I fish). A huge fly, with three long tail filaments. The dun has a cream and dark-banded abdomen and large erect yellow-olive wings, the spinner white and dark-banded

118

abdomen with gauzy blue-black wings. The dun usually hatches in the late morning and afternoon and falls of spent female spinners occur mainly from mid-afternoon to dusk.

Not all rivers have mayflies, and the reasons for their patchy distribution is not clearly understood. Essentially they require very clean water with high mineral salt (especially calcium) content. So they occur on some chalkstreams, such as the Test, but not others; and on some limestone Pennine streams, such as the Aire and Wharfe, but not others. But why not "others" that seem as suitable we do not know. Numbers fluctuate. In some years hatches are sparse, in others huge. Recent years have seen an increase of mayflies, possibly due to a reduction of organic pollution from sewage works. For instance, on the middle and upper Ribble more and more mayflies hatch every year on lengths where they were very rare or did not occur twenty years ago.

Where mayflies occur in large number they can dominate the trout diet and, consequently, angling for most of the late spring period. And so large and unmistakable is the mayfly that it is an instructively useful species to use to illustrate the relationship between the various stages of the upwinged fly life cycle, the trout and the angler.

The eggs of the mayfly sink, after being deposited on the water surface, to the river bed and hatch into the larvula or first-stage nymph. This burrows into the silty sediment where it remains for twelve months (some entomologists have reported a two-year nymph stage), feeding and growing. In this burrow the trout will rarely, if ever, come across the nymph so that it is of no angling consequence. In late spring the mature nymph emerges from its burrow and swims quickly to the water surface where, in a matter of seconds, it moults into the dun. From the nymphal shuck, that suspends from the water surface film, the dun emerges onto the surface film. Trout take both nymph and dun at this stage but the latter being visible is of greater importance to the angler. To fish a nymph underwater when easily imitated duns are being taken is rather pointless . . . ! All that is needed is a good imitative dun pattern, a good cast that does not drag, and stealth so that the feeding fish are not disturbed. So much can the hatch of mayfly duns "turn the trout on" that it can be relatively easy to make a good bag. But the mayfly do encourage the larger trout

119

to feed at the water surface and thus provide the best opportunity in the trout fishing season for the angler to stalk and catch those larger trout. I remember one June day on the River Aire when I was particularly fortunate in this respect.

Once their wings are dry and wing muscles functioning, and provided they haven't been devoured (!), the mayfly duns flutter from the water into the riverside trees and bushes. Here they roost under leaves or in nooks and crannies, and moult into the spinner. Then, one or two days after emerging from the water as the dun, the spinners leave their shelters and join together in mating groups or "dances". The males repeatedly flutter upwards; then with wings held out, glide down in an attempt to out-do the other males and attract a female. Mating occurs, quickly, on the wing and the male's job is done. He falls to the ground, forlornly struggling to remain airborne. The female heads quickly back to the river with her cargo of fertilized eggs. Heading upstream she drops her precious load, a few at a time, into the stream by touching the water with the tip of her abdomen. Then once her abdomen is empty of eggs she too falls, spent. But whereas the male spinners usually die over the land, she often falls onto the water. So the trout have a second mayfly meal, this time of spent female spinners. So attuned can the trout become to intercepting mayfly spinners as they fall, in their death throes, onto the water that I have seen trout actually leap from the water to take a spinner in mid-air. When the trout are in this mood they will take the artificial fly boldly and fiercely: so fiercely that it is worth using a 5 lb B.S. leader point to avoid breakages.

Any river trout angler who has not experienced a mayfly hatch ought to try his hardest to spend a few days on a good mayfly stream at this time of the year. It will be instructive: it will be exciting fishing! But one sad point. I agree with those who, over the years, have recorded that on mayfly streams the fishing deteriorates rapidly once the mayfly hatch is over. Mayfly time is such a time of gluttony for the trout that they appear to become satiated and do not respond as well to hatches of blue winged olives, pale wateries etc. in the summer as do the trout in mayfly-less streams.

Artificial Flies to represent the mayfly:
There are lots of suitable patterns many of which I have tried
over the years.

For the dun: any with a hot orange hackle will do the trick.
I use the Aire Mayfly Dun.

For the spinner: any "Spent Gnat" such as the Aire Spinner.

Medium Olives: small duns, about the size of iron blues, of
a dull olive colour hatch through late spring. The trout take
them but not to the exclusion of other larger ephemeropterans when they are on the water.

Artificial fly to represent the medium olive: Greenwell's
Glory, size 16.

Pale Wateries: these small pale upwinged flies begin to hatch
towards the end of this spring period. However as the bulk
of the pale watery hatch occurs a little later, in late June
and July, I have dealt with them more thoroughly in the
next chapter. The term "pale watery" typifies the divide
between anglers' flies and scientific names, for there are
many similar species within the group "pale watery".

Angler's Curse, (or *Caenis*): again this is not one species but
a group of species of fly, they are tiny pale flies, easy to
identify for they have three tail filaments. Others (except
for the large blue winged olive and huge mayfly) have but
two.

The *Caenis* separate into two nicely distinct types: the evening
Caenis which hatches as a dun in the afternoon or evening and
the morning *Caenis*. The former is the one met by most anglers
who are on the river later in the day. Vast numbers of duns will
emerge and settle on angler and his fishing gear: they can be
an absolute nuisance! Once, in the Outer Hebrides, I had to stop
fishing for they settled in my ears and hair, behind the lenses
of my glasses, down my neck . . . everywhere. Immediately they
moult into spinners (the only upwinged fly that has the dun-to-
spinner moult within a very short time of hatching from nymph
to dun) and swarm, mate and ovulate. The angler who has been

used as a moulting platform will be covered with the empty shucks of the duns once the spinners have emerged. The evening *Caenis* is not only a pest as far as the angler's comfort is concerned but can ruin the chance of reasonable sport. To imitate this tiny fly is, to say the least, difficult! And if one has a potentially good imitation to expect a trout to choose that from the millions (literally) of naturals that will be on the water needs more than a modicum of hope! When the evening *Caenis* is "on", in huge numbers the trout will rarely consider anything else. Fortunately such days are few

It is a different matter as far as the morning *Caenis* is concerned. These hatch around dawn, usually in numbers that, though sometimes considerable, are never so huge as the evening species. And by 10 o'clock on a late spring morning they will have hurriedly passed from dun to spinner phase, mated, ovulated and died. Thus, most anglers never meet the morning *Caenis* for they are abed when it is out! However, it is worth a dawn visit to the river on a potentially hot early June morning to try to experience a hatch of the morning *Caenis*: a slightly larger species compared with the evening form; easily imitated and a good fish-taker. This early morning species is, alas, less widespread than the pain-in-the-neck evening form.

Artificial fly to represent the evening *Caenis*: the Paythorne Caenis, size 18. (Tied on size 20 hook it is as successful as most in dealing with the evening Caenis).

This is a fly devised as recently as 1984. I had encountered a huge hatch of morning *Caenis* at dawn on the Ribble at Paythorne and, except for a suicidal fish that took a tiny Black Gnat, I returned home at lunchtime fishless but with some samples of the natural fly. That afternoon I devised some imitative patterns and was back on the river at dawn the next day. There was another hatch of the morning *Caenis* and my new pattern scored: I had six brownies and a chub. Over the next nine mornings there were further early morning hatches and the new Paythorne Caenis did me proud: altogether it accounted for a further 27 trout.

In the following year (1985) hatches were sparser, but the artificial still caught 31 fish for me. We also tried it out during hatches of the evening *Caenis* with some success. This is one of the handful of occasions when a pattern that I have devised has been really successful!

Large Green Dun:
Brook Dun:
False March Dun: } The "ecdyonurids"
Olive Upright:
Dark Dun:
Yellow May Dun:

Thus far the upwinged flies considered in this chapter have generally a fairly widespread distribution, from the chalkstreams of southern England to the West of Ireland, north of Scotland and north of England. This group, known to scientists as the Ecdyonurids, are characteristically rocky river and stream species of the north and west. They are closely related to that fly of early spring, the true march brown, and the August or autumn dun of late summer (see chapters 8 and 9). Because several members of the group hatch in late spring this seems the ideal opportunity to discuss them.

I have listed the members of the "ecdyonurids" on page 124, together with the peak period of the emergence of the duns. All, except the yellow may dun occur solely in fast rocky streams as are found in upland Britain; the yellow may dun is the only one also to be found in Southern England.

Because of this geographical distribution the ecdyonurids have been somewhat neglected by trout angler-writers, as can be seen easily from a perusal of angling literature. Most members of the ecdyonurids are missing or given scant treatment in the writings of Halford or Skues for they concentrated on chalkstreams where there is only one member of the group. Also Esmond and Lee, in *Brook and River Trouting*, a book published in the midst of the chalkstream 'imitative fly revolution' and which dealt mostly with trout flies on northern streams, also gave them barely a mention. The northern fly dresser Roger Woolley in *Modern Trout Fly Dressing*, (first published in 1932) described a few

TABLE 1
The Ecdyonuridae: habitats and periods of emergence

Dun	Spinner	Main Habitat	Peak Period of Emergence
Autumn Dun	Great Red Spinner	Fast rocky streams and lakes	Aug–Sept
Large Green Dun	Large Green Spinner	Alkaline fast rocky streams	Jun–July
Brook Dun	Great Red Spinner	Fast rocky streams	May–June
False March Brown	Great Red Spinner	Fast rocky streams	May–June
March Brown	Great Red Spinner	Fast rocky streams	Mar–April
Olive Upright	Yellow Upright	Fast rocky streams	May–July
Dark Dun	Dusky Yellow Streak	Fast rocky streams and lakes	June–July
Yellow May	Yellow May	Alkaline lakes and rivers	May–June

ecdyonurids and also included the comment that the autumn dun "is thought by some to be a second crop of march browns."

Of more recent books John Goddard (in the excellent *Trout Fly Recognition*) wrote, of the autumn dun, "hatches are rarely prolific . . . are occasionally welcomed by the fish." Of the brook dun he commented that "hatches of the Large Brook Dun are often sparse,'" of the large green dun "although the fish occasionally feed on them, the number rarely generate much interest," and of the false march brown "a certain aura of mystery still surrounds this species." Roger Fogg (*The Art of the Wet Fly*) and Taff Price (*Rough Stream Trout Flies*) gave them relatively little

PLATE 11

Eric Haygarth netting a trout in a tricky lie on the River Ribble. This is one place where it is essential to wade, but slowly and carefully, if you are to take a fish. The current divides at the head of the pool and the fish lie in the slack water between the two fast-flows.

PLATE 12   DIFFICULT LIES

The lie is beneath the overhanging sycamore sapling on the right bank just above the bridge and in only a foot of crystal clear water. Trees on the left hand bank make the bank cast difficult and on the forward cast the fly often hangs up in the sycamore branches. The main flow is down the middle of the stream so, with the lie beyond the flow, drag is a problem.

A difficult lie because of the need to cast accurately under the very low footbridge which has a log jammed beneath it. The better trout lie on the upstream side of the bridge and thus the fly must land a yard or so beyond the bridge.

treatment, concentrating more on the species of upwinged flies that occur also on the lowland streams despite the fact that both these works dealt primarily with the flies of upland streams. Finally, J. R. Harris in *An Angler's Entomology* (a great book which gives some detail on the group) gave a classic example of ecdyonurid neglect when he wrote that one species, *Heptagenia lateralis,*, "occurs in mountain streams . . . stony shores of mountain and upland lakes . . . widely distributed . . . the duns are very common along the shores of Ullswater, Windermere and other lakes . . . trout at times feed on them. . . . This species has not yet (1952) received any common name, and is here given one" : the dark dun. Can anyone imagine as common a fly occurring on the streams and lakes of lowland Britain not being given a name by trout anglers?

In the Introduction I inferred a certain degree of reluctance on the part of northern trout fishermen until recently to investigate and experiment. They happily stuck to the subsurface general wet fly "deceivers" (hardly "imitators") and did not give much time to studying the insect food taken by the fish. Thus there was a tendency to give all those flies in which the dun is fairly large and of an overall mottled buffish-brownish hue the name "march brown". This clumping was aggravated by the entomologists' house not being in order, as far as some of the ecdyonurids was concerned. It was not until 1931, for example, that the false march brown and the true march brown were separated by biologists and this is a classic example of the problem of treating two similar species as one for angling purposes.

True march browns were (and often still are) described as being abundant flies in the north and west of Britain. Copious patterns evolved to catch fish. However many anglers have considered dry fly ineffective and wet fly more efficient when trout are presumed to be taking march browns. All anglers accept the effectiveness of the wet March Brown as an outstanding general deceiver pattern on lakes (where march browns do not occur) as well as rivers throughout the world. So, when "march browns" were hatching and it was recorded that the dry fly was pretty useless but wet fly effective the following question must be asked: did the trout take the wet March Brown because it represented the fly on or over the water or because it looked

125

like a good general food item?

Now it is clear from the literature, correspondence that I have received and personal research that the true march brown is a very local species whereas the false march brown is a common and often abundant species. There are some who consider that the true march brown has decreased over the past half century: of this I am not wholly convinced. It is far more likely that the more widespread false march brown was confused with the true march brown (as was also the autumn dun and brook dun). However, it is now known that the false march brown nymph does not usually hatch at the water surface in the typical dun manner, but crawls rather like a stonefly nymph onto dry land where it moults. Thus, when false march browns are hatching, and their duns seen flying over the river and fish are feeding at the surface of the water, the fish will *not* be taking false march browns! Hence a dry fly pattern will not be effective though a wet fly may take fish through its general power as a deceiver pattern. I remember well the first time I noticed this, on the Ribble at Henthorn. Huge numbers of false march browns; not one trout would take my dry fly imitation. Then I noticed that the duns were emerging on the shingle; every stone had at least one moulting nymph or empty shuck. Further observation showed the fish to be taking midge pupae or newly hatched adult midges.

There has almost certainly been, in the past, also a confusion between those species of ecdyonurid that hatch in spring and the large olive (*Baetis rhodani*), the most widespread of all upwinged flies. In recent years I have witnessed, many times, the following confused by anglers:

large dark olives called march browns
olive uprights called large dark olives
olive uprights called march browns
brook duns called march browns (and, once, the mayfly!)
dark duns called march browns
dark duns called large dark olives
yellow may duns called march browns
yellow may duns called large dark olive (!)

Such confusion can frequently result in a creel lighter than would be the case without this confusion.

126

The nymphs of the ecdyonurids are all "stone-crawlers"; that is, they spend their lives living under the boulders of the river-bed or scuttling over stones were they graze on microscopic algae. They are very poor swimmers. Ecdonurid nymphs are highly adapted for surviving in the roughest of streams. Their bodies are flattened in the manner of aerodynmic Grand Prix racing cars to allow smooth flow of water over the body with the minimum of turbulence and drag, yet in such a way that the fast flow and low attitude of the nymph, even when moving across the stones, results in the nymph being sucked onto the stones and not swept away by the flow. The legs of the nymph stick out sideways in such a way that the nymph does not have to raise its body high in order to move. And at the end of the legs are strong claws which enable it to keep a firm hold.

That the trout (and grayling) take large numbers of such nymphs is obvious from gut analyses. On the Aire and upper Ribble, where it is possible to watch brown trout feeding through the clear water they can be seen grubbing about on the riverbed, tail up and head down, with fins and tail striving to maintain position as they rummage through the finer stones and occasion-ally swinging downstream to intercept a disturbed prey item. Such a fish has a gut invariably crammed with caddis larvae and ecdyonurid nymphs.

But to imitate these nymphs, which can number hundreds per square metre of stream bed, is by no means easy. Certainly it is a simple matter to devise a leaded nymph that attaches itself to the riverbed : but expensive in hooks and time. Besides which, why should a trout take your single inert nymph as it lies there amongst so many moving naturals? Far better is it, when a fish is seen nymphing in shallow rough water, to fish the nymph to that fish in the hope that it will take the artificial as one that has been washed or grubbed out and is drifting downstream.

The mature nymphs of most upwinged flies float to the water surface to moult into their dun stage. However some of the ecdyonurid nymphs do not. Their nymphs crawls out of the water and moult on the riverside vegetation or boulders. In these the dun stage is of little value to either fish or angler. I have already referred to this behaviour in the false march brown and have also observed it in the large green dun, autumn dun and brook dun. In the latter two I have watched both modes of emergence simultaneously: duns appearing at the water surface whilst others have been crawling up onto exposed boulders and grass stems in the waterside. The most interesting was when I had in view a large number of trout that were lying motionless in the depths of a clear pool whilst at the same time large green dun nymphs crept from the pool to moult. The trout appeared oblivious to this movement. It seems likely that this mode of emergence suggests to the casual observer that the hatches of some ecdyonurids are sparse and not worth the anglers consideration (see, for example, the comments of Goddard "hatches are rarely prolific . . . hatches are often sparse . . . small numbers rarely generate much interest"). However this is not necessarily true. The hatches can be huge though the numbers hatching at the water surface may be small. But even so trout will frequently take such duns in preference to more abundant species which may also be on the water.

The spinner stage of the ecdyonurids is, by far, the most important for anglers. No matter how the dun emerges, the spent female spinners almost always end up on the water. And whereas the dun hatch may be spread over many hours (mid-morning to late evening), the spinner fall occurs in a short period, usually in the evening. Thus the spinners are more concentrated on the water than were the duns. But sometimes there is a problem unless the angler is aware of what is going on: the fish are feeding at the surface, but on what? The spinners lie flat in the rough flow and are usually very difficult to see. The clue, therefore, is to assume that frenetic feeding activity by the trout in the late evening between May and September on upland streams and rivers, and where the natural food cannot be seen, is due to a fall of ecdyonurid spinners. Then trial-and-error, or careful examination of the water surface will usually provide the answer as to the species.

For example, one evening in late May 1982 on the River Lune the trout were going beserk and I could not work out what they were taking. After a frustrating few hours I was removing my waders at the car when my torch lit on the answer. My waders had three dead spent false march brown spinners sticking to them. The next two evenings the fish behaved similarly; I checked carefully in the water. Sure enough, masses of spinners, and with a spinner pattern I caught a lot of trout. On another occasion, also on the Lune, this time in August 1984, my son Peter and I had three consecutive outstanding evenings when there were immense falls of autumn dun spinners. And once more the trout were selective and refused to look at any fly that did not imitate the natural. Furthermore the natural fly, lying flat on the water, was again very difficult to see in the failing light. Similarly on the Lune, Ribble, Aire, Wharfe, Eden, Nith, Annan and a range of smaller northern becks there have been occasions when the spinners of all the ecdyonurid species have provided me with an outstanding evening's sport. And beyond any doubt, the falls of ecdyonurid spinners have produced a response from the fish that has far exceeded that produced by the falls of the spinners of any other upwinged fly save for the mayfly on the northern streams.

The identification of the eight duns and corresponding spinners is not difficult. The true march brown I have dealt with in the last chapter. For the angler and the novice angler-entomologist the duns and spinners of the autumn dun, brook dun and false march brown are so similar that there is little need to separate them. When I discovered the importance of the ecdyonurids on my home rivers I spent a lot of time devising new fly patterns to imitate each species. This was futile, for in trials the March Brown patterns of Roger Woolley that I recommended in Chapter 4 proved more successful than my "Autumn Dun Pattern" and "Brook Dun Pattern". So, treat these as "march brown" if you wish. Alternatively, if you see "march browns" in numbers in March and April, they will be true march browns. In May and June they will probably be false march browns or brook duns. In autumn they will be autumn duns.

The other four ecdyonurid species (large green dun, olive upright, dark dun and yellow may dun) are of similar size to the "march brown types" but have different colourations. These are set down on the next page.

	General Colouration of	
	Dun	Spinner
Large Green Dun	Green	Green
Olive Upright	Olive Green	Yellow
Dark Dun	Olive Brown	Dull Yellow
Yellow May Dun	Golden Olive	Yellow

But once more, following experimental design and testing of artificial patterns to represent these it seems that very few patterns are needed:

To imitate	Large Green Dun, Olive Upright, Dark Dun and Yellow Dun	Dry Flies Greenwell's Glory M.G. Green Dun
		Wet Flies Wet Greenwell's Glory
To imitate	Large Green Spinner, Yellow Upright, Dusky Yellow Streak, Yellow May Spinner	Dry Fly Malc's Special Spinner
To imitate	Nymphs	Woolley's March Brown Nymph Sawyer's Pheasant Tail Nymph

Sedges

In most rivers there are many species of sedges. Some are quite tiny; others very large. Some are dark, almost black, whereas others are of the palest cream or sandy colouration. Several of the larger species have been given English names by anglers, such as the sandfly, Welshman's button, and brown sedge. Many more have no angler's name. But despite this great variety of sedge species, the river trout rarely (never, in my experience but one should never say categorically "never" or -"always" when speaking of things piscatorial) become selective to one species

of sedge. Thus one *rarely* will need different patterns to accommodate what happens to be the trout's sedge-of-the-moment.
Such is completely at odds with what can often be experienced
with the upwinged fly or dipterans, when the fish will take one
fly to the exclusion of others.

I think that there are three main reasons for the lack of selective
feeding by trout on individual species of sedge. Firstly sedges
are rarely as abundant on the water as any of the upwinged fly
or dipterans on which the trout can become preoccupied. There
are rarely on the water numbers of one type of sedge as large,
for example, as when there is a good hatch of mayfly duns or
fall of hawthorn flies. So the trout never become obsessed with
one sedge species. Furthermore it is common to see, during the
better sedge hatches, three or more species of sedge simultaneously. Thus the trout will be accustomed to a variety of size
and tone of the insects on which they are feeding. I say "tone"
and not "colour" because my last suggested reason for the trout's
catholic approach to artificial sedge patterns is that sedges tend
to be most active from dusk through into the night. And, whilst
I accept the trout's greater acuity of vision compared with ours,
I do not think it likely that they can distinguish one species of
sedge from another, in poor light, by differences of shades of
brown. Of far more importance are size, shape, and possibly, tone
of the flies.

Thus, whilst there are many patterns of artificial sedges available to represent the different sedge species, most of the capable
experienced trout anglers I meet carry just one or two patterns,
possibly tied in a range of sizes. So, when four of us are fishing
the same beat, late in the evening, we will all catch trout that
are feeding on sedges even though our sedge patterns differ from
each other, often quite markedly. You can try it for yourself.
Buy or tie six different sedge patterns, go to the river on a good
"sedge evening", and keep changing whenever you catch a fish.
And provided that the shape and size are reasonable then you
will catch with them all: black, brown, cinnamon, sandy, cream.

Sedges that are on the water frequently do not float downstream inertly as do duns and spent spinners. They often "buzz"
on the water, or skitter across the slower pools. Thus the artificial
can, with profit, be allowed to drag across the surface. It is

131

important that the artificial patterns should float really well. For this reason a palmered-body, or spun deer-hair body are best; and well oiled. Offers are usually positive, the fish sometimes hooking themselves as they hurl themselves onto the fly. It pays therefore to use a heavy leader point when fishing the evening sedge: I rarely go below 5 lb B.S.

Pattern to imitate sedges:
For the reasons given above I recommend either a Deer Hair Sedge or Black or Brown Palmered Sedge, sizes 8–12.

Sedge activity is particularly affected by the weather. On cool, blustery or rainy evenings few will be out. What is needed, ideally, is a still warm humid evening for then the sedges may be on the water to midnight and beyond.

Dipterans

Late spring sees a great proliferation of dipterans, some of which, on occasion, can dominate the trout diet. Possibly the two best known, and possibly most important are the hawthorn fly and the black gnat. These are very close relations, the hawthorn fly being *Bibio marci* and the true black gnat *Bibio johannis*. Several other black land flies are sometimes given the name black gnat.

In some years very few may be seen around the river, but in others huge numbers might be out in the valley and in strong winds will find their way onto the river. The most incredible "fall" of hawthorn flies that I have ever seen occurred in May 1985: the riverside pastures and trees swarmed with them. And so many were there that, with the stiff breeze, the River Aire was kept constantly supplied with them for three days so that the flow resembled a conveyor belt carrying literally millions downstream. The fish ignored all other flies. And so abundant were the natural flies that our artificials were generally ignored amongst the majority of real flies! And so abundant were they that the fish fed for small spells and, once their stomachs were full, went down satiated. It was frustrating knowing that we were hoping that the fish would take ours from the hordes, yet the long odds were against. Still, we managed to catch and, at the same time, try out a range of patterns. The two offered below are excellent whenever black flies are on the water:

132

Dry Fly: Hawthorn Fly (size 12 if hawthorn flies are "on",
   sizes 14 or 16 for smaller species)
Wet Fly: Black and Peacock Spider (size 12–14)

The first falls of dung flies or terrestrial beetles might also
occur in late spring, but generally these are not as important as
in summer (See Chapter 8).

Finally small midges (chironomids) are ever with us and if
nothing more substantial is on the water the trout take great
delight in taking these and ignoring our larger more traditional
artificials. How to catch trout regularly that are feeding
exclusively on the tiny midge that abounds on the rivers I fish
is a problem I have yet to solve. I have had some success with
a tiny (size 18) Grey Duster, and an even tinier (size 20 or 22)
Titchy Midge. But not enough success to boast about. In late
spring such occasions are rare, for there are generally a lot of
large naturals on the water which can be represented by good
artificials which the trout are only too obliging to take. If you
fish often enough you will encounter midge-dominated days and,
like me, have to suffer. Such days are good for the soul and give
plenty of opportunities for nature study once you have given
the fish best.

CHAPTER 8

The Dogdays of Summer : Mid-June to Mid-August

"After the beginning of July the angler may have a pleasant day's fishing though his basket will not often be heavy."
Lord Grey of Fallodon. *Fly Fishing*. 1930.

Come mid-June and river trouting changes, often quite dramatically, from a time of bountifulness to one of potential arduousness. Even the riverside alters, as if in sympathy with the angling.

In *most* years the period through summer is characterised by periods of prolonged drought and low water. What rain falls is generally soaked up quickly by the parched soil or evaporates quickly as a consequence of the dry atmosphere. Similarly the plant growth in the valley reaches its zenith in this period. So roots absorb their maximum volume of water which passes, through the vascular tissue of the plants to the leaves whence it evaporates from the leaf stomatal pores in the transpiration stream. Thus, except in the wettest of British summers (of which more later) river levels are kept low.

Long bright summer days result in high water temperatures which should be expected to result in high metabolic rate of the river inhabitants. However, there is a problem with very high water temperatures. The higher the water temperature the less amount of oxygen that can dissolve in the water. Thus there is less oxygen available for the trout and their aquatic invertebrate food supplies to use in the manufacture of energy. So, the trout frequently appear lethargic during the heat of the day. Many anglers will have witnessed this—trout lying in the pool but a fly cast over them is completely ignored. The pool, in which only a few days or weeks earlier there was an abundance of fly life on the water surface and keenly-feeding trout, now appears listless and lifeless.

Life around the river seems, through the long summer days, less conspicuous and less active than was the case through spring. By the end of June most spring flowers have faded and are setting seed. These are replaced by meadowsweet, willow herb and others that appear less fresh and bright than the earlier blooms. In periods of drought the spring greens of pastures and meadows are transformed into dull olives and straw browns.

Even the waterside birds seem lethargic. Most species have completed their breeding cycles by the end of June for yet another year. Woodland species move into the uppermost tree canopies where there is an abundance of insect larvae. Ducks shelter amongst the riverside rushes, drab and camouflaged in their eclipse plumage. Waders quit the riverside once breeding is complete, taking their newly-fledged chicks to the coast where they will spend the winter. No longer do we hear the territorial songs and calls so characteristic of spring. No longer do we see birds flying to and fro with nest material and food for their growing chicks.

Through the heat of the summer dog-days the riverside is uninviting and best left alone by the trout fisherman. In any case, during the daytime the riverside becomes attractive to that other sort of human, the day tripper, who chooses to form traffic queues at the narrow road bridge and spend the day with the family paddling, swimming, canoeing and stone-throwing in the most accessible trout pools. It can be quite depressing, for the newcomer to river trout fishing, to come across such disturbance on the pools that he was hoping to fish. But the experienced trout angler does not bother too much for he knows that when the day-trippers leave, in the evening, the trout will emerge from their hiding holes amongst the water side alders and amongst the boulders of the riverbed. And then, well into the hours of darkness they will be catchable.

It is always a good basic rule, in trout fishing, to fish when the trout are feeding. In early spring that means in the early afternoon. In the second half of spring fishing might be possible from just before dawn, through the day and well into darkening. Of course, depending on the day. But in typically hot summer conditions the trout will come onto feed as the sun falls and may, if the night remains still and warm, continue to feed through to beyond dawn. And that is often, at this time of year, when the trout angler should be on the river.

During the heatwave of August 1981 I spent a week trout fishing on the River Nith in Dumfriesshire. The river was showing its bones: boulders usually submerged at normal river level protruded. The bigger pools had but a sluggish flow and the best of the streamy runs were but shallow trickles. Through the day the sun beat down mercilessly, penetrating the clear water to the riverbed. With stealth and my polaroids, I scrutinised the two miles of river and saw nothing but a few fearless parr and a school of small stale sea trout in the larger pool.

As evening fell I sat, despondently, on a high bank overlooking a long shallow pool tail. A spash, then the bow-wave as a biggish fish forged upstream through the thin water. Then another. Then several more. Possibly sea trout, for they will run even in low water? But no! they were brown trout. And they were not "running" upstream as do sea trout but emerging from beneath a line of riverside bushes and trees on the opposite bank and moving out to take up their nocturnal feeding stations. Several I followed as they left their dark seclusions amongst some willow and alder roots that grew into the river margin, and spashed their way to their chosen lies. And then they began to feed on the red spinners of the August dun that were trickling, spent, downstream. Within half an hour an apparently fishless river was transformed, and I had a successful evening.

The rest of that week I turned out in the early evening and fished through to dawn when the fish returned to their daytime low water lies. Each night followed the same pattern. At dusk there was a fall of spinners and then, when darkness really took hold sedges and moths spluttered and crash-landed on the surface. Then, around dawn there were small hatches of duns and another fall of spinners. So I "matched the hatch" and changed dry flies as necessity dictated. I kept two or three better fish each time and returned the rest.

Those nights, and I have had numbers of other similar summer nights over the years, I fished dry fly. This may puzzle those who have never fished dry fly in the darkness, when the dry fly is difficult to see even with a full moon.

One has an advantage at night in that the fish are usually bolder than they are during the day. Thus one can approach much closer and see clearly the splash of the feeding trout. Given low river banks, or sparsity of trees over-hanging the river, one can often see the artificial fly (usually a large bushy sedge) as it drifts downstream only a few yards away. It takes a bit more concentration than is the case in daylight. But at night extraneous parts of the surroundings are hidden from view and one's sensory system becomes incredibly focused on the job in hand. A hedgehog snuffling in the riverside undergrowth, the grunt of a roe deer, the short bark of a fox, the screech of the tawny owl—these can be off-putting certainly in the first few all-night expeditions in search of the nocturnal trout, but after a few nights' training one seems to mould oneself into the natural history of the riverside. Indeed, I often feel when fishing during the day that I am an intruder or, at best, observer of the riverside creatures. Yet at night I become one of them! It may sound daft to those who have never spent a night on the river with only the valley animals for company. If you think I am exaggerating re-read this paragraph, and then read Hugh Falkus's *Sea Trout Fishing*. Then go night fishing on the river.

Even on the darkest nights, when one cannot see the trout feeding and one's dry fly, it is still possible to catch trout. Even on dry fly. For one can listen for offers rather than look for them. This takes a bit of practice. But when a trout takes a floating sedge imitation it does so with a slightly more splashy sound than when it takes a natural fly. So the object should be to find the feeding trout by ear, judge distance by touch, and listen for the offer. This is as big a challenge as one can hope to find in angling. But remember, the sensory system is hyperactive when one is out in the wild darkness of night. The adrenalin flows. With the body thus attuned it is amazing what we can perceive even without thinking about it. Once, for example, in pitch darkness on the River Aire I cast to a fish that had risen sometime earlier. The cast was unsuccessful. But then I suspected that the fish had moved upstream of me. I cast to it, lifted the rod and hooked it: a brownie of 2 lb 11 oz. Did I see the fish? Surely not. Did I hear the fish? Well, it did not make a splash. A sixth sense maybe—Most experienced anglers can recount such tales.

Not that one needs to fish the dry fly. In fact one might be as well fishing wet fly through the stream until one has got the hang of night fishing. And, because one cannot see the subtle indication of offers that come to upstream fishing, cast across and down the stream, feeling for offers. Smaller fish will predominate, but even the larger wild brownies will take wet fly that are dragging a little at night. They are just that little bit more foolhardy than they are in the day. Neither are they as selective (unless they are feeding on blue winged olives).

If one's casting is up to it then fish two or three flies: if not then stick to one fly. There is nothing so frustrating as having to unravel tangles at night; and the use of droppers predisposes to tangles if a cast is at all faulty or during windy conditions. One must stumble from the river, find the torch and then, having sorted out the mess, discover that one's night vision has been ruined by the light.

Orange Partridge (which adequately represents the drowned spent spinner of the blue winged olive), Waterhen Bloa (to represent other olives) and either William's Favourite or Snipe and Purple will make up a suitable three fly evening cast. All size 14 or 16. And if, during the day, pale wateries have been on the water then a size 16 Yellow Partridge can take its place on the cast. But once the light has gone completely then a bigger more bushy wet fly can be profitably used either singly or on the top dropper to represent a sedge or moth. A Brown Palmer, Black Palmer, Sedge Pupa or, if a more traditional fly is needed, a large bushy Coachman or Woodcock and Yellow will suffice: tied in sizes 8 or 10.

At night trout will take such wet flies violently. So a 2 lb. or 3 lb. B. S. leader point will just not do. Personally I would never go less than 5 lb. B.S. at the point when night fishing. I have known sea trout up to 11 lbs. and salmon up to 16 lbs. irrationally take such flies both day and night.

Even the best caster will occasionally find his leader tangled or get caught up in a riverside hawthorn bush. So it is a good idea to have, already set up, several spare leaders with flies attached on cast carriers. Then should one find the leader in a "bird's nest" it is a quick and simple matter to snip off the lot into a spare plastic bag and attach a new one.

Two words of warning—firstly make sure that no nylon is left when you go. Discarded fishing line is the curse of riverside creatures. They have more right to be there than we anglers have; and to be responsible for the death of any bird, mammal or whatever due to carelessness is reprehensible. Furthermore, such behaviour brings the name of angling into disrepute.

Secondly if you do get "hung up" do not pull against the rod. You run the risk of breaking it. Pull line off the reel so that it is not bent. Put the rod under your arm (not on the ground or you will stand on it in the dark). Hold the slack line beyond the tip ring and pull on that. Tackle dealers make a lot of profit from anglers who thoughtlessly value their flies and leader more than their expensive fishing rod.

Finally, whatever you are doing at night by the river my advice is to do it more slowly than you would do in the day. To stride boldly across the shingle makes a racket in the quiet hours and you are likely not to see the big rock waiting to trip you up. River banks appear steeper at night: take them slowly. Barbed wire fences can be invisible at night. Our ability to perceive distance is poor at night. Knots are more difficult to tie in poor light, even with the aid of a torch. Tie them slowly and test them before you lose a fish. And above all, make sure you know where you put things down by marking them with white fish cloth. When you are walking along, rod in hand, always carry the rod handle-first: you are less likely to break it by prodding the tip into the ground or a tree trunk.

There are some waters where one cannot fish the night through. Day-ticket waters usually where anyone can go and buy a ticket. Generally on these beats angling is restricted to the hours from sunrise to one hour after sunset. For most of the year this is fine but given a heatwave this imposed rule means that essentially the angler has just one or two effective hours and for the most of the day has to sweat it out in the hope of finding one or two suicidal fish. But no matter how hard he works the angler's best chances will be that last session which is artificially brought to a halt by the rule.

Generally I prefer, myself, not to fish this type of water. But

139

once or twice each year I pay a call on the Bolton Abbey Estate Water on the beautiful River Wharfe. The day ticket allows fishing from 9.00 a.m. to one hour after sunset, so a dawn session is out. Then through the heat of the summer day the river is invariably assaulted by thousands of day-trippers who seek the outdoors, sun and river. Few pools have no children paddling and splashing about. Canoeing regattas stream down the river. But come that last magic period and a visit is still worthwhile for once the people have left the river the fish appear, as if by magic!

John and I purchased tickets on such a day and waited until the day-trippers had left the pools were undisturbed and in cool shadows and a few sedges and mating spinners danced under the trees. We spun a coin for pools: I lost and strolled off down stream.

A fish moved in the body of the pool under an overhanging sycamore, where not long ago people had swum. A pale watery dun fluttered on the flow and was taken with a swirl. Quickly I removed the Orange Quill (I had expected a fall of spinners) and tied on a Norris' Pale Watery Quill. The fish took on the third cast and soon I had it in the net. As I slid it into the creel another, seemingly better trout, took a fly in the pool tail. I crept downstream and watched. Twice, in quick succession it rose. My Pale Watery Quill was ignored but in the meantime the trout continued to feed. I tried a Greenwell's, again with no success, and an Orange Quill. Then I tried a small size 12 Brown Sedge and it took first chuck! A big fish which made several strong runs downstream before I could bring it in: it turned out to be a rainbow trout of 3 lb. 1oz., in perfect condition.

Several British streams, though not "stocked" deliberately with rainbow trout have these resident in them: the Spey, Aire, Wharfe, Dove are some such. These are, of course, descendants of escapees from fish farms. In most rivers the species never really establishes itself but in the four I have mentioned it spawns and thrives. Wild rainbows are quite distinctive when compared with those produced by fish farms by the absolute perfection of their fins and their distinctive subtle colouration which stock fish rarely have. Beautiful creatures!

After the capture of the big rainbow trout time was short. All

140

along the river fish were feeding in the gloaming. I missed one by my over-eagerness but then had two more, smaller brownies of about a pound each as I strolled back upstream.

Time to pack up! John had had five brownies and kept four, the biggest of which scaled just over two pounds. We had our limit each and all taken in the last hour of the day.

Some nights it is a waste of time staying on the river through the night: nights when, after a clear hot day, the air temperature falls soon after sunset, mist swirls down the river and a heavy dew falls. I think that what happens on such evenings is that the sudden fall in temperature forces the flylife to shelter in the riverside vegetation so that there is nothing on the water for the trout to feed on. Such evenings are all too common in the streams at the heads of Pennine valleys or in the higher Scottish glens.

Peter and I had one evening like that in the Outer Hebrides: a hottish day, warm evening and then a mist-laden chill after sunset. The fish "came on" as the sun sank behind the mountains and "went down" half an hour later with the dank mist. We also had a day on the Upper Wharfe when the mist appeared shortly after the sun fell behind the western fells: the fish were active for only ten minutes when the sedges were active. So it pays, when planning a night's trouting, to choose one where the weather forecast does not threaten too great a fall in night air temperature compared with the day. Especially if the trip involves a longish drive: a round trip of 100 miles is bit frustrating when rewarded by only a few minutes potentially profitable fishing.

A lot of through-the-night anglers have taken brown trout when sea trout were intended quarry. I once had a fine 3 lb. 11 oz. fish on the Spey on a size 2 Medicine in a bag of five sea trout. Likewise, on some rivers at least, sea trout often feature in the bag of brown trout. And often the sea trout are seen to take a natural fly before the artificial. I have had sea trout, up to four pounds, on the Nith, Annan, Hodder and Ribble on tiny dry flies at dusk. And, of course, some "sea trout flies" are also good brown trout wet flies. Wet Black Gnats, Orange Partridge, Waterhan Bloa, Snipe and Purple: these will often take both species at night, especially in low water. Indeed, one of the best anglers I have ever fished with, John Dixon, said to me (of sea trouting on the Nith)

> "When you see brownies feeding, fish for them. The sea trout will be in with them."

And, to prove the point, the following evening he had a bagful of grayling, brown trout and sea trout (to $2\frac{3}{4}$ lbs) and all on size 14 and 16 trout wet flies!

Thus far it might be imagined that the only way to catch trout in summer is between dusk and dawn. This is not so. But over the years I have found that I stand a better chance at night than I do in the day in hot low water conditions. Certainly on spate streams. Often on chalkstreams.

However, given an undisturbed private length of river with a deep fast flow and plenty of cover in the form of weed beds (usually water crowfoot) or overhanging trees, some fish will continue to feed during the hottest of days. However the fly hatches can be sparse or non-existent in the midst of such days and thus the available food will be in the form of nymphs, caddis larvae, shrimps and water hog-louse. So some trout will be feeding in the depths with often no sign of activity at the surface. The problem then is one of finding the feeding fish.

Some anglers try to overcome the problem by "fishing the water": an exhausting, hot and sweaty way to go about it. More effective is to cast, with a wet fly or nymph, into likely places: weir pools, dark holes beneath trees etc. But the best solution is to find the fish! All that are needed are a pair of polaroid sunglasses to remove the glare from the water surface, extreme stealth and patience.

To stomp along the bank wearing a white tee-shirt will mean that you have done your bit for fish conservation. They will have fled as you approached. Drab clothing. Hands-and-knees crawling "on your belly" may be required. And slow, very slow movement. Trout can take some spotting, especially when lying among fronds of weed. So time must be given for careful scrutinising of the river bed for the tell-tale shape or the sideways movement and white flash of the mouth opening as a trout intercepts a food item. Finally, most important of all, the cast must be as delicate and accurate as possible with the minimum of false casts.

To take such extreme care can often make the difference between an outstanding day and a complete and utter blank.

I once spent two hours in the blazing sun sitting by a pool on the River Aire which I knew would hold at least one sizeable fish. The pool is only about ten yards long and the river no more than four yards wide at that point. I then saw the fish move: a good brownie it seemed. It was lying under the overhang of the opposite clay-cliff bank with just its pectoral fin on the right side showing. But occasionally, it would move a matter of inches, out into the main flow, to take a food item. I waited until it was safely on its lie and flicked my size 16 Sawyer's Pheasant Tail Nymph about a yard upstream of it. I could see the nymph as it sank and drifted down. The fish seemed to be ignoring it! So I raised the rod and the nymph accelerated and rose through the water as it passed, a few inches from the fish. The trout reacted by slowly gliding out of its lie and down to the nymph which was now only a couple of yards from me. As the trout's mouth opened, then closed, I raised the rod. What a commotion ensued! The shocked fish tore off downstream, taking all the slack line and more from the reel. Slowly I persuaded it to return and eventually had it in the net. My best fish ever from the Aire at 3 lb. 3 oz.

That was quite a few years ago: and by that experience I learned the value of both patience and stealth.

Of course it may be that there is some fly on the water and that the trout are willing to rise to the dry fly despite the heat and brightness of the day. But save for the pale watery dun and midges few aquatic species emerge under such conditions. More likely is it that land based dipterans either fall or are drifted by a warm breeze onto the water: dung-flies, daddy-long-legs, ants. One should be especially prepared for such falls when riverside meadows are being mown, for this type of operation invariably disturbs large numbers of insects and with a favourable breeze many will find their way onto the river. It is obviously impossible to forecast such happy events. But if one is planning to be on the river through hot days it is important to be prepared.

Once I arrived on the banks of the River Eden on a sweltering mid-August morning. Not a thing stirred. Then at 11 o'clock a clanking sound proclaimed the arrival of farm machinery in the meadow to take the last cut of grass for silage. By noon the dry easterly wind began drifting daddy-long-legs, that had been hiding in the sward, out and across the river. Many, possibly damaged somewhat by the farming operation, fell onto the water and the fish responded. A day in which I had expected to have to work hard for the odd fish was transformed into a bonanza! Fish were still feeding as I left. Yet close to the bridge where I had parked the car, only half a mile away, the river was still lifeless, unaffected by the fall of daddy-long-legs.

On another occasion, this time on the River Wenning, I encountered the only big fall of winged ants that I have ever seen. Through the morning not one fish moved, but at 2 o'clock everything changed. The riverside vegetation swarmed with ants and they fell, in huge numbers, on the flow. So many were they that my dry fly imitation was greatly outnumbered and I could entice only two trout. But without the ants I am sure I would have had a blank day, certainly before evening.

The other source of insect life falling into the river and which might encourage trout to feed in even the hottest, brightest weather are overhanging trees and bushes. In fact it is a useful ploy when conditions are very arduous, to creep up to an overhanging tree and give it a good shake. Some insects or spiders are sure to be dislodged and fall onto the water and, maybe, encourage some fish to rise. I suppose the real purist might throw up his arms in disgust at such a suggestion. But it often works. Once a friendly horse, that had an itchy nose, performed the task for me. That should be fair enough! Yet many potential food items will fall, from time to time of their own volition. So when one is desperate it is a good ploy to sit on the river bank opposite some overhanging vegetation and wait. Only one fly or beetle may fall during the afternoon; but if a trout is aroused and takes it then that fish is catchable and should be yours.

Another useful ploy in lies that are overhung by tree branches, especially of oak, is to plop a good green caterpillar imitation onto the water. Oak trees, especially, are hosts to many types of moth larvae some of which pupate, in late summer, by lowering themselves on silk threads to the ground into which they burrow. If the tree overhangs the river then some lower themselves into the water and the trout become accustomed to this easy source of food. Some years are almost plague years as far as this caterpiller-oak relationship is concerned: 1969 and 1978 were two such. One August afternoon in the latter year I watched as scores of these suspended caterpillars gently dropped from an oak tree into the River Lune. And beneath that one tree I caught several fish, all on a caterpillar imitation.

Thus far I have referred to trout fishing in summer during hot drought conditions. Of course in most years such periods are broken by periods of heavy rain, and in others, thankfully few, the summer is persistently wet. 1985 was one such, when the rivers in Northern England and Scotland were almost constantly above summer level from June to September as Atlantic depression followed Atlantic depression without respite. What a contrast that was after 1984 when barely a drop of rain fell between April to September. And although high water spate conditions can occur at any time through the fishing season it is high summer when they are possibly most welcome for the trout angler and have the greatest impact on trout fishing.

Once the river begins to fall and no longer carries big items of rubbish the trout will emerge and seek food. However, though there may be sparse hatches of fly at this early state of the clearing spate, the fish will not take them. They become preoccupied with food items washed out of the land by the flood: earthworms, slugs, beetles etc. Or, under cover of the coloured water they prey on lesser fish that are sheltered out of the stronger current: minnows, miller's thumbs; even parr of their own species.

At this state of the spate the angler is in a dilemma. The most effective way of catching trout is to use bait or an imitation of what they are feeding on. Logically, then, the use of a worm might be considered legitimate or the natural minnow. Alternatively, an artificial spinner in the form of a small spoon, quill minnow or "Mepps" may be effective. But on many trout waters today such fishing methods are prohibited by the fishing rules. Where the rules stipulate fly only yet allow any form of "fly" then one or the larger lures will take trout that are feeding on small fish. A size 10 or 12 Peter Ross or Silver March Brown is ideal, cast into the quieter water just out of the main current and tweaked slowly back. A sinking fly line can be used to advantage to get the fly down to the fish which, in high water

145

tend to feed deep, close to the river bed. Frequently the use of this method has yielded for me trout on days when, looking at the river, one would have imagined that angling was a waste of time. One such, on the Ribble stands out particularly well.

The river was just falling from a very big flood and bays of slack water were formed at the edge of the field. The water was coloured a light brown. I sat, in the sun, by one of these bays. Then amongst the emerging grass stems I saw a swirl: a fish had moved in, probably, no more than six inches of water. I drifted a dry fly, then wet fly, then nymph over the shallow bay to no avail. Looking through my box of wet flies I found a small Peter Ross, tied it onto the leader and cast it across the water. Then I slowly tweaked it back. In the space of no more than five minutes I had three trout to the net, one of which, a good fish of 1 lb. 8 oz., I kept. Moving downstream I fished four other similar bays where the river had inundated the meadow and caught several more including chub. Back at home I examined the stomachs of the three trout I had kept. One contained five minnows and three earthworms, another seven minnows and two earthworms, and the third had four minnows, two miller's thumbs, a large black slug and two earthworms. Not one contained a nymph, larva, dun or other insect.

Incidentally when fishing these slightly larger flies in spate conditions one should use stronger leaders: certainly no less than 6 lb. breaking-strain. One can get away with it for the thicker leader is less visible to the trout in the murky water. But also sea trout and sometimes salmon will take such a fly in these conditions and, should this happen, one must have tackle that can, at a pinch, handle such quarry. Tales abound of such captures. Recently a 28 lb. salmon was landed on a size 12 March Brown in a falling spate of the River Nith. The lucky angler was after sea trout and brown trout. Possibly more remarkable was the occasion on the River Hodder when an angler, who had fished to no avail for salmon throughout the day, turned to his trout fly rod for the last hour before the darkening. He immediately hooked and landed a 15 lb. salmon on a size 14 Orange Partridge!

Once the river has fallen considerably following a spate then the silt begins to settle and the water quickly clears. Then trout fishing can be conventional. Fly hatches may be large throughout the day so that dry fly will score heavily. Alternatively the angler may prefer to fish the subsurface wet fly or nymph, especially if the fish are taking nymphs or other insects from beneath the water surface. This opportunity to fish during the day in high summer when there is a lot of fish activity, should not be missed, for it contrasts with the more usual pattern in low water summer conditions when the dusk to dawn period is best.

Flies of High Summer

Hatches of aquatic flies and falls of land flies in high summer are as diverse as the hatches of spring but generally are not as large nor predictable in their timing. Many species the angler will have met earlier in the season (e.g. sedges), others have their main hatches in this period such as blue winged olive. So it is imperative the angler keeps his wits about him in this most diffi-cult time of the year. He must be constantly on the lookout for a fall of one species of land fly, or a hatch of duns or a fall of spent spinners; or, on the most difficult days, trout that are nym-phing deep in the pool. And, of course, he must have in his fly boxes imitations to cover every possible fly or situation he might meet on the river. It is all too easy to go home fishless in the dog-days of summer.

It is difficult to make a comprehensive list of *all* the natural flies on or in the water at this season. So, in the list that follows, I will include those that invariably appear each year, those that appear most years, and some that might appear on the water only occasionally but when they do appear the trout go berserk!

Sedges: see Chapter 3, pp. 61–62 and Chapter 7, pp. 130–132. The major hatches and activity of sedges occur in the period from sunset to midnight, sometimes to dawn. Larger more prolonged sedge activity occurs on warm still nights than cold wet ones.

Pale Wateries: the term pale watery encompasses several species, more than one of which may occur on one length of river. The differences between the species are subtle and one need not imitate such subtle differences in the artificial flies that one uses in the various hatches of pale wateries.

147

Essentially pale watery duns are small or very small flies with wings about 1 cm. high (or long). The body colour may vary from almost white, through shades of cream to, at the darkest, the palest of olives. The dun may hatch at any time between dawn and sunset, the time depending upon air and water temperature, and light intensity. In hot weather and low water the cool of dawn and dusk sees the biggest hatches, whereas in higher water and cold overcast weather the main hatches may be in the middle of the day.

The pale watery spinner, known as the "amber spinner" has a bright amber-orange coloured body that, in bright light, gleams and almost glows. Mating and egg-laying occurs late in the day or just around dawn so that a fall of spent female spinners may occur at dusk or after sunrise.

There are many good artificial flies to imitate the various species of pale watery dun. From trying most of them and inventing a few experimental ones I would recommend the following:

Dry flies to represent the pale watery dun	Tup's Indispensable, Norris's Pale Watery Quill, Malc's Special. Sizes 18, 16 (most useful) and 14.
Wet flies to represent the pale watery dun	Yellow Partridge, Poult Bloa.

To represent the female spinner during a fall on the water after egg-laying I would commend my own Orange Spinner. Sizes 18, 16 (most useful) and 14.

Blue Winged Olive: a famous trout fly which has the reputation of being difficult to imitate successfully (i.e. when trout are obsessively feeding on blue winged olives it is said they will rarely take an artificial). It is an easy fly to identify, for it is the only medium-sized river fly with three tails. So does the smaller *Caenis* and larger mayfly. But the duns of all other river upwinged flies have just two tails. The blue winged olive has an olive green body but, as in most species, there is variation. Sometimes the body may be almost brown in colour. The wings are, as the name suggests, a distinct blue-grey. In early summer the blue winged olive dun hatches in the late evening but, as the season progresses or when temperatures fall, hatches occur earlier, sometimes around noon.

The blue winged olive spinner is known as the sherry spinner because of its bright rich amber or golden brown sherry body colour. The main falls of spent spinners occur, following egg-laying, in the late evening. It seems curious that, during hatches of blue winged olive duns, a dun imitation is sometimes less successful than a blue winged olive spinner pattern. Once for example, on the River Hodder during an afternoon hatch of the duns I tried every olive green dry fly pattern in the box (eleven different ones!) to no avail. Then I had three fish in quick succession to my Orange Spinner pattern. So if, during a hatch of blue winged olive duns you find this happening, try a spinner pattern just in case. And whereas for most trout flies just a couple of artificials will suffice, it is worth carrying several for the blue winged olive to provide a wider choice just in case the trout are being particularly fastidious.

Dry flies to represent the Blue Winged Olive dun.	Greenwell's Glory (tied with an olive silk body), Olive Dun, Jacques Blue Winged Olive. Size 14.
Wet flies to represent the Blue Winged Olive dun.	Poult Bloa, Olive Spider. Size 14.
Dry flies to represent the Blue Winged Olive spinner	Pheasant Tail Spinner, Orange Quill, Orange Spinner. Size 14.
Wet fly to represent the Blue Winged Olive spinner	Orange Partridge. Size 14.

August Dun: one of the ecdyonurids or "march brown types" that occurs only on the rivers and streams of northern and western Britain. A fairly large fly with wings about 2 cm. in length with a superficial colouration reminiscent of the true and false march browns and brook dun of spring (see Chapter 7, pp. 123–129). The spinner, likewise, is known as the red spinner, being clumped by anglers with the spinners of these other four closely related species.

From my experience the duns often hatch in fits-and-starts over a long period, and they may hatch like others in this group by crawling from the river rather than hatching at the river surface. Thus the August dun is of minor importance as a trout fly. However the falls of female spent spinners can be huge; such falls occur in the late evening, often through to well beyond midnight. Should one have opportunity to use profitably a dry or wet fly to imitate the August dun during a hatch then the march brown patterns given in Chapter 6, pp. 108–109, will be suitable. For the spinner I would recommend the Orange Spinner, sizes 14 or 12.

Small Dark Olive: a small very dark olive, the same size as the Morning *Caenis* and smaller pale wateries. But it is much darker than these, the dun being a dark olive brown with grey wings and the female spinner dark reddish-brown. In cool weather the dun hatches in the afternoon, but in very hot weather the hatch occurs as the temperature falls at sunset. Female spinners may be found on the water in the evening.

To imitate the small dark olive is not difficult

Dry fly to represent the dun	Greenwell's Glory (tied with olive silk body) or Kite's Imperial. Size 16 or 18.
Wet fly to represent the dun	Waterhen Bloa. Size 16.
Dry fly to imitate the Dark Olive spinner	Pheasant Tail Spinner. Size 16 or 18.

Midges: though midges may be active on or over the river at almost any time of the year it is mainly in the summer and autumn that the river angler is sometimes blackmailed by the trout into accommodating imitations of them in his armoury of flies. Throughout spring and early summer there are usually sufficiently large hatches of bigger, more conventionally imitated flies that the fish will take. But come summer and there can be days when the fish will look at nothing that is not a midge! So vast are the numbers of species of midges that it is impossible to describe them all. But, as with sedges, two or three adult patterns to represent the green, black and orange species will suffice. It is this general body colouration and the size of the natural fly that the angler should be prepared to match from his natural fly box.

Firstly let me suggest pupa patterns. One might try tiny wet flies of appropriate size and colour such as Olive Spider, William's Favourite and Orange Partridge tied on size 18 or 20 hooks. These *can* be successful. However, over the past two seasons I have had more success with Suspender Buzzers (patterns taken from stillwater trout fishing) tied on sizes 16 or 18 irons. The advantage of these is that, being suspended on the surface film, they behave more like a hatching midge pupa and that one can see the offer clearly in the manner of dry fly fishing.

For dry representation of the adult midges I would recommend my own Titchy Midges, tied in different body colours and on hooks 16, 18 (probably the best all-round size) and smaller. As a more general pattern that scores heavily, sometimes, there is none to beat the Grey Duster, size 16 or 18.

However, no matter how may patterns of flies you carry, more often than not life will be difficult when the trout are feeding solely on midges. So you will have to work hard in such circumstances to get a good bag.

Black Gnat: falls of these occur, as in spring (see Chapter 7, pp. 132–133).

Reed Smut: a tiny black dipteran only a tenth of an inch or so in length which can occur in droves on the water. When this happens fishing will be difficult. Very difficult. Hope that you will never encounter smuts in the numbers that affect trout feeding patterns. And if you do try the smallest black flies in the box, and pray.

Miscellaneous land flies: most anglers will be able to recognise most land species that might fall or be swept onto the river in summer. The following are those most likely to occur from time to time:

Ants: red and black varieties. Have a couple each of the Red Ant and Black Ant in the corner of the fly box. Just in case!

Beetles: there are vast numbers of beetle species in Britain, any of which might attract the trout's attention when, during population explosions, they find their way into the river. Many earlier writers devised special patterns to cope with particular species of beetle, the Welsh Coch-y-Bonddu being possibly most famous. This is, in fact, a good general beetle pattern. Alternatively one could have a range of cork beetles, which are easy to tie and can be painted to cover a very wide range.

Moths: these can be important in heavily-wooded valleys on warm summer evenings. The Coachman or Brown Moth are good general patterns. Or a big sedge pattern might do the trick. For I am sure that the trout will treat moth and sedge as one if they are on the water.

Daddy-long-legs: these hatch from riverside pastures and meadows in huge numbers from July onwards. Any good dry fly pattern will do, that devised by the late Richard Walker being excellent.

Dung flies: all anglers or countrymen will be familiar with these hairy brown flies that occur in swarms around cowpats and in riverside grasses on hot summer days. They are frequently blown onto the river and the trout take them keenly. A size 12 Wickham's Fancy is the best medicine for this land fly.

Caterpillars: as explained earlier these can be especially important in pools where tree branches overhang the water. In summer, therefore, it is worth having one or two imitations, just in case. I use my own Green Caterpillar.

During June, July and August the aquatic life of the river is at its most active. So patterns to represent nymphs, larvae and crustaceans are important. Fortunately only two patterns are essential:

Sawyer's Killer Bug
Sawyer's Pheasant Tail Nymph

Tied in sizes 10–16 and with various amounts of wire ballast, to give different sinking rates, these are essential.

Finally can I re-emphasise three points, for having the right flies in the box is one thing. The most important aspect is having the right fly on the leader when the trout are feeding. So

1. Try to fish when the fish are feeding;
2. Take care when approaching the feeding fish;
3. Take time watching carefully so that you choose the most suitable fly to match the natural food.

These are important throughout the trout season. But especially so in the high summer.

CHAPTER 9

Season's End: Late August and September

"For many seasons . . . I had not fished for trout there [on the Itchen] during September, having found September trout increasingly easy as the month advanced. . . ."

G. E. M. Skues. *Itchen Memories.* 1951

Many river trout anglers disregard the last few weeks of the season. Some argue that the trout that remain in the river are too close to spawning and that they should be left in peace. It is true that as autumn comes trout rapidly develop their bright yellow and red-brown mating livery, and the ovaries and testes enlarge. Only a greedy angler would take numbers of such fish. However it seems a pity to avoid trout angling in this interesting last part of the season: the angler can always use barbless hooks and return the fish, unharmed, to the water if they seem too close to spawning. In October the trout rod must be put away for the long six months of close season and there is no real merit in voluntarily prolonging this period of celibacy.

It is also argued by some anglers that few reasonable trout remain in the river beat at the end of the season. Such is usually completely untrue. In fact there are often more catchable trout in a particular beat through the end of the August and September than was the case a month earlier. in July. With the first rains of autumn and the cooling of the river, brown trout begin to move upstream towards the headwaters and sidestreams where spawning will occur. So, in a well-positioned river beat just downstream of the spawning grounds, hundreds, if not thousands, of trout will slowly pass through. And as they feed keenly, preparing for the breeding season, so they can be caught. Amongst these running fish will be very large specimens that have spent the months following the previous breeding season further downstream. Possibly they will have summered in beats where trout fishing pressure is light or where fishing is primarily for salmon. Possibly some will be "slob trout", large brown trout that have dropped to the river estuary for the summer where they have fed on shrimps, prawns, crabs and fish fry in the brackish tidal water. The last part of the trout season gives the angler the chance to try for one of these larger fish.

So, whilst many anglers turn to the prolific autumn runs of salmon or turn to the grayling for sport in this early autumn period it is worthwhile having a few last days with the river brown trout, even if most or all have to be released.

A few years ago I spent two September days on a beat of the upper Lune. In July and early August this beat had held few trout of any real size. But things had changed. Every run, every stickle held at least one trout and the two deeper pools held scores. In the two days I caught many fish, all over the pound mark, and the best 3 lb. 13 oz. (which I kept). All these trout had moved into the beat from the primarily salmon and sea trout beats further downstream. Similarly in a falling spate on the Upper Ribble, in August 1979, a mass movement of brown trout occured on the last stages of a spate. In a matter of days the beat was transformed from one with few fish over the pound mark to one with large numbers of fish up to two pounds (I caught one fish at 2 lb. 12 oz.) in four days. On yet another occasion, this time on the Aire, the two largest trout of the season, both well in excess of the three pound mark, were caught in the last few days. Certainly these had not been in this tiny stream through the season.

Season's end, therefore, gives you chance to catch the really big wild trout that have eluded you throughout the year. But also, as the weather cools and rainfall increases as autumn advances, the fishing regains a more sociable, settled pattern. The heatwaves and droughts are gone. The cool evenings do not encourage hatches of fly, trout to feed and the angler to stay on the river to ungodly hours. We see more of a spring-time pattern with hatches of fly in the late morning and afternoon. We

155

can have a leisurely breakfast, have a splendid day on the river, and yet be home for tea with no real intention to tarry longer.

The actual timing of the often abrupt change from the temperamental style of the dog-days of summer to a settled autumn routine varies from year to year. In hot summers with prolonged droughts it may be the beginning of September when the Azores High, that has dominated for so long, is overcome by a series of Atlantic depressions. So it was in the famous heat-waves of 1975, 1976, 1983 and 1984. But with more typically "mixed" British summers it may be mid-August when the change occurs. And in really wet and cold summers, most recently experienced in 1985, there is no abrupt cut-off point: end of summer—start of autumn. There really is not a summer and we have to contend with a continuation of the high rainfall/high and coloured river that has dominated the year. Given very dry or "normal" British summers and I think that it is the onset of continuous cooler weather and prolonged higher water that encourages the pre-spawning movement, upstream, that I referred to earlier.

For the angler who has persevered throughout the season there are now few pitfalls as far as imitating the natural foods of trout is concerned. Indeed, the end of the season is marked by the welcome return of the two favourites of early spring: the iron blue and the large dark olive. It is almost as though the latter, referred to in Chapter 6 as the "spring olive" appears to remind us that the new season is barely half a year away. On upland rocky streams hatches of that close relative of the march brown, the autumn dun, reach there peak. It will be recalled (from Chapter 7) that Roger Woolley commented that some considered the autumn dun to be a late hatch of the march brown. And as the autumn dun and its spinner (the great red spinner) are so similar to the local hatches of spring march browns so it too reminds us of the beginning of the seasons gone and to come.

Some flies that appear on the water at season's end are the remnants of the summer hatches. But as I have pointed out, these hatches are now more predictable as to their timing. Blue winged olives, medium olives, a sprinkling of pale wateries: these will emerge from their nymphal stage in the early afternoon provided that the weather is not too inclement. And given a warm Indian summer in September there will be falls of spinners and sedge activity in the later afternoon.

There is only one group of insects that the angler must be aware of in the last few weeks of the season and that he is unlikely to have experienced earlier. And it is a group that has received very little publicity. Greenfly!

At the end of the trout season, the greenfly population on the leaves of riverside trees (especially, it seems, sycamore) reaches a peak. With the first leaf fall of autumn, or leaves being ripped from trees by the early autumn gales, many leaves end up in the river with greenfly still attached. One such leaf may harbour hundreds of these tiny insects. So, as they are washed from their leaf the trout begin to take them. In a remarkable year there may be so many greenfly in the river that the trout become addicted to them. The fish soon learn that these dainty food morsels are associated with the big flat green or autumnal brown structures and they will seek out the leaves floating downstream and take greenfly from them. To an observer the trout appear to be nymphing at first sight. But if a good vantage point is gained and the water clear the antics of the trout are quite clear. It is almost as if they are playing "heading the ball" with leaves!

That a good greenfly imitation is essential when the fish are up to this trick can be seen from autopsies: two trout I killed from the upper Ribble in September 1984 were so full of greenfly that they were dribbling out of the gills and a 2 lb. 8 oz. fish from the Eden in 1983 had 679 identifiable greenfly together with a huge mass that were partly digested. For the grayling fisher in early October and November the problem of coping with such fish becomes greater as leaf fall reaches a peak.

Two flies, both regarded as "fancy" grayling flies will score heavily when trout or grayling are taking greenfly:

dry fly: Grayling Witch, sizes 18–20
wet fly: Green Insect, sizes 18–20

There are other greenfly imitations available; I have devised one or two for myself. But from trials none seem to work as well as these.

Whilst on the subject of "fancy flies" I can recommend three more that, for some strange reason score heavily in the end of the trout fishing season. Again they are traditional grayling flies, but have taken some of my best autumn brownies:

Red Tag, size 14: both wet and dry flies
Treacle Parkin, size 14: dry fly
Sturdy's Fancy, size 14: dry fly

Certainly they are close enough in general appearance to suggest arthropod (insect or crustacean). And they often score more heavily than imitative patterns at this time of the year. Possibly the coloured tag provokes a violent response from the trout that, at this time of year, are at their most aggressive due to the accumulating sex hormones. Whatever the reason, the Red Tag has given me several trout around the three pound mark in northern rivers where a two-pounder is a good fish whilst on the Lune I had one of 3 lb. 1 oz. on the Sturdy's Fancy in 1982 and on the Eden a headstrong cock brownie of 3 lb. 4 oz. on a Treacle Parkin in September 1985. In each of these cases the fish had been seen to take duns from the water surface but had refused my more conventional patterns.

For some anglers the end of the season comes as a relief. Exhausted they crawl away for six months of civilisation before the next onslaught. For others there are feelings of great sadness, for yet another year is over as far as the important things in life is concerned. For many the end of the trout season is but a signpost in the year: for there are still grayling and salmon waiting to be caught and some wildfowling trips on the estuaries of northern England and southern Scotland. But the end of the season is a time of reflection and mental preparation for the next.

On the 30th of September I like to sit on the hill overlooking one of my favourite northern trout streams. The days since the start of the season pass through my mind: the failures and the successes. They seem such a long time in the past. And when I get home I check through my diary. And from this short period of reflection emerges a list of jobs to do, questions to be answered, problems to be solved. It is always a long list: of waters to visit next year, of scores of flies to tie, of new leaders to make, of rods to be rewhipped or varnished, of reels to be overhauled, of lines to be greased.

158

CHAPTER TEN

Hard Days and Difficult Lies

"Many and varied are the reasons assigned by anglers to account for meagre results of a fishing expedition. Some of them are reasonable and readily understood and appreciated by other anglers though unintelligible to less favoured mortals. . . ."

R. C. Bridgett. *By Loch and Stream*. 1922.

Throughout this book I have deliberately chosen instances, from my diaries, that illustrate how a particular technique, certain fly, type of approach etc. can turn an unproductive situation into one that is successful in terms of fish landed. And at the outset of this chapter I must admit that I have done what all angling writers do, quote successful days when a lot of fish were caught and ignored times when the result was zero. A blank. A fishless day. How can any self-professed expert admit to others that he, like them, sometimes fails to catch!

Too often readers of angling literature are led to believe that if they mimic the well-known angling writers then they too will be able to follow set formulae and catch a lot of fish every time they take the fly rod down to the river.

Far from it!

I will be honest with you. Like every trout angler who is out from the opening day to the final day of the season, and who ventures forth no matter what the weather once, twice, thrice or even more times each week, I have fishless days. Such days are much more common in the early years of one's career. Even the legendary G. E. M. Skues was a slow starter:

"It is gratifying to know that Skues' total bag for the 1874

159

season was but two trout, proving to us lesser mortals that he was not born with the skills that he was to demonstrate in later years."

Donald Overfield. *G. E. M. Skues: The Way of a Man with a Trout.* 1977.

No. The earlier years of anyone's river fly fishing career will be marked by many failures and many blank days. Many of these will be due to sheer ignorance of technique or knowledge. Sometimes almost stupidity!

May I describe the sort of thing I mean; an early embarrassing blunder on my part?

Being a "northerner" I was raised with the northern wet fly, fished as by local custom down and across the stream and worked back against the current until the team of three flies hung below me in the flow when another cast was made. I had caught quite a lot of trout by this method: they had all hooked themselves. I thought that this self-hooking was the norm.

An expedition was planned to the superb Settle Anglers' water on the upper Ribble where, I was told, the fish were waiting to give themselves up. "But take some dry flies!" I was advised.

I bought some dry flies from the local tackle shop and took them, with my trusted wet flies, to Settle. I had never fished dry fly before.

I caught nothing through the morning on my wet flies and then, in the afternoon, there was the biggest hatch of duns that I had ever seen. The trout took them eagerly. The trout ignored my wet flies. "So," I thought. "Time for the dry fly!"

I knew from something that I had read somewhere that I was supposed to cast the dry fly upstream to rising fish and this I did. Nearly every time I cast to a trout that I had watched take a dun there was a splash and my dry fly disappeared. But not one trout hooked itself. No one had ever told me that one had to tighten to set the hook to offers to the dry fly! So I had a lot of offers. I should have had a lot of trout. Today in the same circumstances I would. But that day I had a blank! (Having written this I am now blushing with shame. Honestly. But I was only a lad at the time.)

I soon learnt. Mostly by reading as much as I could about my trout fishing obsession. By talking to other anglers I met by the river. By watching anglers who were obviously much better than me. By copying the ways of others. Is that not how we all learn the basic rudiments of the sport?

However, whilst one can learn from others how to cope with *many if not most* situations on the river, No one can ever nor will ever be able to tell one how to cope with *every* situation. Thus there will be days, hard days, during which even the greatest angler will be defeated. There will be lies in the river, difficult lies, from which even the greatest angler will be unable to extract a trout.

Why?
Well. Some of the reasons for failure have already been mentioned in earlier chapters and suggestions made as to possible solutions that have worked in most cases. But they might not work in some cases: on some days, with trout in some lies.

Why not?
Well. We are dealing with a set of living organisms (trout and their foods) together with an environment that is constantly changing in time (water temperature, light intensity etc. vary from day to day) and in space (very rarely are two trout lies *exactly* the same along one short length of river). It is not a mathematical equation or engineering problem where, if one follows a set of rules, one always gets a precise result. Because something works on one day or in one place does not mean that it will necessarily work on the next day or in the next place.

So we have our broad general patterns. The ones I have talked about in the previous chapters of this book. We apply these but then we have a blank day or find one trout in one lie that we cannot catch. We sit down and analyse the situation and look hard for possible reasons for the failure. Then we suggest one or more solutions. Should we come across that problem again we can try out the solution that we formulated the last time. If we are successful then we have gained in experience. If not then we go back to the drawing board. By so doing we have become a better angler. But we will continue, throughout the rest of our angling lives, to meet new strange problems and thus we will never be able to catch every trout in every river on every day. Thank goodness! Even today, well over a thousand days' trout fishing since my elementary dry fly blunder, I still manage to have one or two complete blanks in a year. I still come across the occasional trout that I cannot catch yet only a few yards away are several that I can catch!

E. R. Hewitt (in *A Trout and Salmon Fisherman for Seventy-Five Years*, 1948) suggested that fishermen go through three stages. When they take up the sport they want to catch as many fish as they can. Then, when this becomes a bit mundane. they want to catch the biggest fish. Eventually that too palls and then they want to catch the most difficult fish irrespective of size. Alas very many anglers seem never to pass out of the first two stages. It is with fish in the third category that this chapter now deals. Catching difficult fish! Hard days are easiest to explain away.

1. *There are no fish in the river!*
Well, you will struggle if there are no fish there! But this can happen for natural causes, certainly on the highest rough streams. After spawning during the winter trout tend to drop downstream to deeper water and they begin to return in May and June. It can be quite frustrating, therefore, to visit in early spring a length of stream where there were scores of large trout at the end of the last season and find the water in perfect order but no trout. Once you get to know your rivers well you can predict the time of arrival of the trout in the upper reaches and be ready for them. But many anglers miss out. They go to the stream before the fish have returned, have a blank and never visit the length again. Yet a day, a week or a month later it can be full of fish.

A classic example of this is a two-mile beat of the upper Lune. To catch or even see a trout there in March or April is noteworthy. But from late June to the end of the season the beat is alive with trout. Good trout. And few anglers are aware of it (or were!).

In some waters that rely on stocking for a head of trout then, if the water has not been stocked fishing will again be very difficult. Obviously. I think that it is common knowledge that the bulk of stock-fish are removed by anglers soon after stocking and that the quality of fishing (in terms of numbers caught) then deteriorates. It is quite interesting to note that as this happens so too do the number of visits made to that water by anglers!

162

I will leave you to draw your own conclusions. There is also the sad possibility, as I explained in Chapter 6, that in very early stockings on some spate streams the entire stocking might move downstream, out of the beat and be lost to those who stocked them. That is just one of those things, I am afraid.

The worst cause of a lack of trout is pollution from farm slurry pits and silage clamps, from industrial "accidents", from road accidents involving chemical tankers, sometimes even by deliberate criminal addition of poisons such as cyanide to a river by poachers. Once, as I was tackling up by the Ribble near Clitheroe the local police drew up. "An accidental discharge of cyanide upstream. Don't go fishing in the Ribble today!" And downstream they sped to carry the sad news to farmers and other anglers.

It may not be your fault when you have a blank day!

2. *The fish are not prepared to feed!*

This one *is* your fault As I have explained in earlier chapters usually the trout will feed at certain times of the day but not others. When trout are not feeding they can be the very devil to catch; when they are feeding you ought to catch. Occasionally I have met anglers leaving the river just as I am arriving, on a blazing August late afternoon, bemoaning their lack of success; yet a couple of hours later in the evening the trout are going berserk!

Try to ensure that your hours of fishing coincide with the feeding-times of the trout.

3. *The fish are feeding but you cannot catch them!*

Alas, this is the usual cause of my blank days! Usually the offending food item is a tiny midge that is too small to be realistically imitated and the trout will look at nothing else. Many times Geoff Haslam, Peter and I, often accompanied by other anglers, have sat by a pool on the Ribble, Spey or Wharfe, and tried fly after fly after fly. One suicidal fish has been taken and its stomach contents confirmed our suspicions: full of a grey slimy ooze which, down a microscope, is seen to be a mass of semi-digested tiny midge pupae or adults.

I suspect that the problem is two-fold. Firstly it is difficult

163

to tie a fly small enough to imitate these satisfactorily: even on size 24 and 26 hooks! Secondly the hatch can be so large that our artificial fly is but one amongst many.

The latter is certainly the problem when there are huge hatches of the tiny evening *Caenis* and, sometimes, massive falls of hawthorn flies or ants. The only thing to do is persevere.

4. *The fish are feeding on a fly for which you haven't a suitable imitation!*
You should carry patterns that will cope with most expected situations. However no-one can be prepared for all eventualities. But make sure that you accommodate that particular food item with an imitation in the fly box as soon as possible so that you will be prepared in future. You might have to devise your own fly, especially if the natural fly is of such local distribution that none has been produced before. That is how I came to devise my Paythorne Caenis (pages 74 and 122).

5. *The fish appear to be feeding but you can't see any food on or in the water!*
This is a fairly common event. Use a hand-net or look very carefully and you might find the answer. It could be spent spinners, invisible as they lie flat on the flow; these are notoriously difficult to see in the evening (see page 59). It may be very tiny flies, smuts, greenfly, midge pupae . . . but a hand-net should provide the answer.

But sometimes there really is nothing in the way of trout food! Yet the fish are dimpling the surface. Darting this way and that, apparently to take a food item from here, then from there. You try them with dry fly, wet fly and nymph to no avail. You might even see them shy *away* from a weighted nymph as it approaches them. Such is a not uncommon behaviour of recently stocked trout.

Put on something a bit startling. A big wet fly such as a Black and Peacock Spider or a big bushy sedge and work it faster than you would when fishing for wild trout. Persevere. Change flies if you have to. When, hopefully, you catch one kill it and spoon it. Many times, when I have done this, I have found the stomach empty or containing just bits of leaf, twig, alder catkins, pebbles or horsetail segments.

Not all stock fish behave this way. The more abundant the natural foods the sooner they begin to feed properly. But I have met this quite difficult problem six times in the last five years, so it is not that rare. Such fish can be caught easily, by stripping wet flies or big dry flies through the water. However this is lure fishing and not proper river trout fly fishing.

Difficult lies are a different matter

You have been catching trout when, suddenly, you come across one that you just cannot catch. (Alternatively you may start the day with a fish you cannot catch in which case go and try to catch some others. Otherwise you can't be sure that it is not a "hard day" problem.)

The temptation is to hammer away at that fish with fly after fly after fly. You might be lucky; you might not. Peter once spent over three hours with one trout that was taking mayflies on the Aire. On what must have been well over the hundredth cast it took! I have done likewise. So did Halford.

> "For an hour or more I kept on throwing steadily, and, I am vain enough to think, without making any glaring mistake, over this fish. Commencing with a very small yellow dun (Flight's Fancy), then trying in succession a blue-winged olive, red quill, ginger quill, hackle-winged red spinner, Jenny Spinner and detached Badger, I at length, as a last recourse, put up a small silver sedge on an O hook. The first cast secured a trout upwards of 2 lb."
>
> F. M. Halford. *Dry Fly Fishing*. 1889.

Note: So much for imitative dry fly fishing, Mr. Halford!

But where is the merit of hammering away in this manner? Are we not, possibly, just goading the trout into taking something that increasingly irritates it just as a salmon angler may concentrate with his fly on one fish until it takes? Something must have been wrong for the trout not to rise to the fly very early on in the confrontation. And if we are catching fish elsewhere on the beat that are feeding on the same food items as the fish that is being so awkward then the problem is unlikely to be our imitative fly. But note: I say *unlikely*.

Difficult lies may be a consequence of:

1. *We, or someone else earlier, have disturbed that fish!*
Frightened fish are difficult, if not impossible, to catch. They may lie there in the water, in full view. But the way they lie is less settled than ones that have not been disturbed. Their fins vibrate more quickly, their body quivers, they hug the river bed tightly. They may rise to take a natural fly, but when they do they do so more nervously, more jerkily and less leisurely. The answer is to go away and find another fish, approaching this one more cautiously. Later return, stealthily, to see if that one has settled down.

A lot of anglers do not appreciate that their heavy-footed approach loses them a lot of trout.

2. *The fly may not be fishing properly in that lie!*
This is a common cause of a lie being difficult and it is usually because of "drag". Sometimes the drag may be so slight that unless you watch carefully you don't notice it.

Try casting from further downstream so that the fly line is carried downstream more parallel with the flow and less across it. Try casting from the other bank (if you can). Try casting a very slack line so that drag is postponed whilst the current is taking up the slack. Try plopping the fly lightly right into the trout's window. If these fail go and try elsewhere for another trout. But return at intervals. Watch and think. Persevere, but don't just keep hammering away. Remember that trout in the more difficult lies are often the best trout. They are the ones that other anglers have not been able to catch.

3. *Floating Leader Syndrome (see pages 94–95) may be a particular problem in that lie!*
You should always treat the leader point with sinkant before making a cast to a fish in a new lie. Pay particular attention to this in lies where the water flow is flat and even for F.L.S. is more marked in such lies.

4. *The lie may be a difficult one to cast into properly!*
The best lies often are. I know many such lies, under low foot-bridges, and beneath overhanging straggly bushes and tree

branches that seem to reach out to grab your fly, lies that hold a lot of trout, invariably good trout, which are ignored by many anglers who are not confident enough of their casting accuracy or who are not prepared to risk losing a few flies. Indeed, I have been told: "We ought to root these bushes out!", or "Can't we get Chris to bring his chainsaw?" Yes. But remove this cover and the lie will probably be no more. The trout lie there partly because of the cover.

One such, on the River Aire, is a classic example of this sort of lie. You have three options. To cast a long accurate line into a gap upstream of the lie and allow the fly to float downstream for several yards beneath the overhanging tangle, or aim the fly so that it hits a sycamore leaf on the forward cast and drops straight into the lie. Miss the leaf and you lose the fly and disturb the lie. Demanding exciting fishing. The third option? Ignore the lie!

5. *The fish in that lie is an "educated" trout!*
It may be that the trout in that lie has been caught before, possibly several times, and is thus more perceptive of the difference between an artificial fly and a natural fly.

But note: It is not uncommon, certainly on heavily-fished stocked rivers, to catch a trout that has one or two flies already in its jaw having been hooked before and broken away. Alas, it is also not uncommon on such waters to catch trout that have damaged mouths consequent to heavy handling by previous captors. Anglers who handle fish so badly ought to be banned from the sport. There is no excuse. Another argument in favour of the barbless hook!

So it is clear that it takes a lot of teaching of most stock fish for them to become "educated" to the stage where they will refuse a standard artificial fly.

It may not be a matter of education. It may simply be that the trout is in a lie that allows it more time to scrutinise the artificial fly. In very fast rough water lies one never meets this problem. The trout *must* grab the fly a split second after it appears in its window. But in a deeper slower lie, especially one in the open away from cover where the light is good, the fish may have several seconds to examine the fly as it sails through. Often I have watched fish in such lies rise and turn away at the last moment. I have known that F.N.S. was not the problem; the pattern was probably reasonable to a point for I had caught fish elsewhere on it that day; I had not disturbed the fish.

Following the recommendations of John Goddard and Brian Clarke in their book *The Trout and the Fly*, for such fish I now carry a series of upside-down, parachute-hackled, winged dry flies tied on Swedish Dry Fly Hooks or J.G. Upside-Down Hooks. These are more fiddly to make so I reserve them for such difficult trout (some anglers may like to try them for all their dry fly fishing). Thus the artificial has no hook bend or point resting on or in the water. The parachute hackle spreads in three dimensions (as do the legs of the real fly) rather than just one at the head end. The body lies flat on the flow. The wings of the dun will appear to the trout above the fly in dun patterns and in spinner pattern flat on the flow. It is a style of dry fly that is indispensible on the slower lengths of clear-water streams.

This applies only to fish when they are feeding selectively at the surface on duns, spinners, sedges etc. When they are feeding deep on larvae, nymphs or crustaceans a standard Pheasant Tail Nymph fished with an induced take will suffice provided that the size, shape and action of the nymph is correct. Thus as an alternative solution one could try the difficult "educated" trout with such a deeply-fished nymph. This sometimes works even though the trout is actually taking flies from the surface.

One such lie, in which the trout are generally larger than the standard from this water, is on the River Eden. Though they rise well to natural duns, spinners and sedges, they are reluctant to take artificial dry flies. I once managed to get one on a sedge in the late evening and have had two on an upside-down Green Dun. However trout in this lie (that always hold a fish) are very susceptible to the nymph and the way that they take it is always the same. The nymph is cast upstream. Quickly it sinks and slowly drifts, close to the river bed, down to the fish. A slight lift of the rod and the nymph rises and falls, flickering, as it passes the head of the fish. No response. It seems as if this too is going to fail. Then, just as the nymph drifts past its tail the trout turns, swims leisurely a couple of feet behind the nymph and then quietly takes it. A white flash appears and then disappears as the trout opens and closes its mouth. The rod is raised and the fish hooked. I have landed several fish from this lie by this method (average 1 lb. 9 oz., the biggest 2 lb. 2 oz.) and the take is always the same. But each time it succeeds I am taken by surprise and get a feeling of elation—far more so than when I hook more trout in easier lies.

It is the hard days and trout in difficult lies that make river trout fishing that bit special. For they are the occasions that help the angler accumulate experience, something that no angling writer can do for him.

CHAPTER 11

The Future

Angling is a superb sport and river trout fishing, for many, is perfection. From the tiniest burn set in spectacular and remote Scottish mountains and the high moorland beck of northern England, through the wooded stream of Wales and the West Country to the placid chalkstream of southern England trout fishing is associated with the best that the British countryside can offer. It is a sport that offers peace and tranquility. It demands patience yet provides excitement. It requires observation, reasoning and problem-solving yet provides relaxation. It is one of the oldest sports with a wealth of literature. Such being the case, is it any wonder that trout fishing is so popular?

The last few decades especially have seen a boom in trout angling, mostly led by the revolution in reservoir fishing. Increasingly anglers who live within easy reach of trout streams but who started to fish for trout on reservoirs are turning to rivers so that most clubs and associations close to big urban connurbations have full memberships and growing waiting lists. Good trout rivers are in high demand, again especially those close to larger centres of population, so that the costs of buying or renting a quite ordinary beat are rising rapidly—far more rapidly than the Retail Price Index. This is likely to continue for, as one beat is bought by a fishing club or association (and is never likely to re-appear on the market) so the amount of river that *might* appear for sale in the future diminishes. So we have a situation where more and more people are chasing less and less river.

To cope with this demand more and more rivers are being stocked with more and more trout. Indeed, to find a river that has never been stocked but supports a head of wild trout one must go to the remoter corners of Britain or to rivers that are primarily salmon rivers where the wild brownie is ignored. In most rivers there is a sensible stocking policy that aims to maintain a head of trout appropriate to the size and productivity (in terms of food production) of the water. However, there is in some areas a tendency to have a put-and-take stocking policy so that the head of fish is kept artificially very high. In these rivers the frequent addition of stock fish means that there are always many trout that have not grown accustomed to river life—hardly a satisfactory situation for the river fly fisherman.

One of the most interesting developments that is likely to occur in future years, and one that will relieve the pressure on existing trout streams, is the conversion of coarse fisheries or waters that, at present, hold no fish, into trout fisheries. Coarse anglers will hold their hands up in horror at this and understandably so. However, the cleaning up of rivers that is happening at present in many parts of the country is producing water that can easily support trout. What riparian owner is going to rent his water for coarse angling if he can obtain more income by renting it out for trout fishing? Friction is likely to occur between conflicting interests of coarse and game anglers: local fishery committees will have to deal with this! But to give an example from my home region. The River Calder (a tributary of the Ribble) was, to all extents and purposes, an open sewer for most of its length and a coarse fishery along most of the rest until the North West Water Authority modernised the sewage treatment plants along the river. The outcome has been that this water has now the potential as a trout stream; even salmon and sea trout, that formerly hurried past Calder Foot to the clean upper Ribble, are now running up the Calder. Given time and further river improvements by Water Authorites there is no reason why river trout fisheries should not be spread throughout lowland Britain where there is high demand but a very limited supply.

Some might say that I am exaggerating. I am not! I am expecting that, as we ruined so many rivers in the years following the Industrial Revolution, we shall return most of these rivers to their former glory and that means trout water quality. I know that pollution is still a problem on many rivers but the stronger stand being taken by Water Authorities and local fisheries committees is slowly meeting with success. It is up to anglers to lobby the powers that be to ensure progress continues.

The greatest threat, not just to trout fishing but all angling, is from the anti-blood sports brigade aided and abetted by some factions of the mass-media. Such bodies should realise that the quality of the river valley is a result of the care lavished upon it by field sportsmen. Without the shooting there would be no well-maintained grouse moor or pheasant coppices. Without the angler there would be no trout or salmon in the river—they would have gone through neglect, for in an island such as ours management of such resources is essential. But rationality has never been a virtue of a blinkered bigot. We even have one political party that is opposed to field sports though at present (because of the electoral clout the $3\frac{1}{2}$ million anglers carry) the leaders of that party have no plans to abolish angling.

Yet should a minority will to ban one field sport be successfully imposed it will be just the start. No fox hunting. Next no shooting. Next? Next my friends, no angling. This is a battle we must be prepared for in the future.

In a hundred years time none of us will be here. At present we are holding, in trust, the sport of river trout fishing for future generations to enjoy just as we enjoy it. We owe it to them who will come after us to preserve it and to improve it. We should all give our backing to the organisations, both local and national, that fight our corner in the battles of pollution, poaching and politics. Support your local fisheries committee (the regional Water Authority or your club secretary will be able to provide details). Join the Salmon and Trout Association, Fishmonger's Hall, London EC4R 2EL and The Angler's Cooperative Association, Midland Bank Chambers, Grantham, Lincolnshire NG31 6LE. You owe it to your sport.

Postscript

No angling expert, no angling article, no angling book can tell you how to catch fish every day you go to the river. There can be many reasons for failing to catch: often the word "reason" is the wrong word. Excuse would be better. We anglers have all been making excuses for an empty creel since the sport of angling was invented centuries ago. But to others we cannot use the word excuse; reason, suggesting logic, is the appropriate term. I finish this book therefore with a list of reasons for not catching fish. I would commend you, dear reader, to learn this list by heart. In the long run it might help you when you return home to your long-suffering family. It might help when, with other guests, you are tempted to drink too much in the fishing hotel after a long offerless day. It is as comprehensive a list of reasons as I have come across; written many years ago by Gen. Sir Percy Feilding K.C.B. whilst staying at the Hirsel, Coldstream. I am grateful to Lord Home of Hirsel, not only a major statesman of his century but a splendid angler, for allowing me to pass it on to you.

Reasons to Account for Want of Sport

written down on Upper Bower Table
by Gen. Sir Percy Feilding K.C.B.

1. The River is waxing.
2. The water is too black.
3. The wind is no' in the right qurt.
4. There's a fog on the river.
5. There's mist on the hills.
6. There's thunder about.
7. The glass is falling.
8. The weather is too warm.
9. The fish have been too long in the water.
10. It is too stormy.
11. There are too many white clouds about.
12. She is too big.
13. She is too sma'.
14. She is too dirty.
15. She is too clear.
16. There's too much sun.
17. There's too little wind.
18. The wind is too gusty.
19. There's going to be a change in the weather.
20. The fish are not settled after the flood.
21. The man at the thick end of the rod is a duffer.
22. The thistles on the bank get in the way of the fly.
23. The fisher is in love and not minding his business.
24. The flies are too big or too sma'.
25. There's too many leaves falling.
26. There's too much grue on the river.
27. There are no fish.
28. There has been no spate to clear the rocks.
29. There have been too many waxes and the fish are no' settled.
30. There's a bad light on the water.
31. There's too much snaw brae in the river.
32. It's o'er gurly.

174

I am going fishing now so I must leave you. I hope you have enjoyed reading this contribution to trout fishing; maybe we will meet on the river. I wish you success in your angling. May it never be o'er gurly for you!

References

AELIANUS, Claudius, *De Animalium Natura*, 2nd. Century A.D.

BARKER, Thomas, *Barker's Delight, or the Art of Angling*, 1657.

BERNERS, Dame Juliana, *A Treatyse of Fysshynge with an Angle*, 1496.

BRIDGETT, R. C., *By Loch and Stream*, 1922.

DAWSON, Kenneth, *Salmon and Trout in Moorland Streams*, 1928.

EDMONDS, H. and LEE, N., *Brook and River Trouting*, 1916.

FALKUS, Hugh, *Sea Trout Fishing*, 2 Ed. 1975.

FALLODON, Lord Grey of, *Fly Fishing*, 1930.

FOGG, Roger, *The Art of the Wet Fly*, 1979.

GAY, John, *Poems on several occasions, containing Rural Sports*, 1720.

GODDARD, John, *Trout Fly Recognition*, 3 Ed. 1976.

HALFORD, F. M., *Floating Flies and How to Dress Them*, 1886.

HALFORD, F. M., *Dry-Fly Fishing in Theory and Practice*, 1889.

HALFORD, F. M., *Dry-Fly Entomology*, 1897.

HALFORD, F. M., *The Dry-Fly Man's Handbook*, 1913.

HARRIS, J. R., *An Angler's Entomology*, Rev. Ed. 1956.

HEWITT, E. R., *A Trout and Salmon Fisherman for Seventy-Five Years*, 1948.

HILLS, John Waller, *A History of Fly Fishing for Trout*, 1921.

HILLS, John Waller, *A Summer on the Test*, 1930.

KITE, Oliver, *Nymph Fishing in Theory and Practice*, 1963.

MACAN, T. T. and WORTHINGTON, E. B., *Life in Lakes and Rivers*, Rev. Ed. 1972.

MASCALL, Leonard, *A Booke of Fishing with Hooke and Line*, 1590.

MOORE, T. C., Kingsmill, *A Man may Fish*, Rev Ed. 1979.

OVERFIELD, T. Donald, *G. E. M. Skues: The Way of a Man with a Trout*, 1977.

PRICE, S. D., *Rough Stream Trout Flies*, 1976.

PRITT, T. E., *North Country Flies*, 1886.

RANSOME, Arthur, *Rod and Line*, 1929.

RITZ, Charles, *A Fly Fisher's Life*, 1959.

SAWYER, Frank, *Keeper of the Stream*, 1952.

SAWYER, Frank, *Nymphs and the Trout*, 1958.

SKUES, G. E. M., *Minor Tactics of the Chalk Stream*, 1910.

SKUES, G. E. M., *The Way of a Trout with a Fly*, 1921.

SKUES, G. E. M., *Nymph Fishing for Chalk Stream Trout*, 1939.

SKUES, G. E. M., *Itchen Memories*, 1951.

WOOLLEY, R., *Modern Trout Fly Dressing*, 3 Ed., 1950.

Index

NOTE: For ease of use all artificial trout flies are indexed under Flies, artificial, and all natural trout flies and trout foods under Trout, natural foods.